ARE YOU READY FOR THE LABYRINTH?

You can reach a truly divine state only when you learn to face past emotional upheavals, become responsible for your actions and reactions, and once and for all accept the cycle of life that includes death. This journey is called the Labyrinth. And it can only be traversed through the knowledge and balance provided by the Goddess.

Maiden, Mother, Crone offers the lost but vital connection with the Goddess in all her diverse and glorious myths and archetypes. Meet Siren, Ceres, Freyja, and others whose symbolism you can now personally interpret for strength, growth, and understanding in twentieth-century life. You'll become reacquainted with your individual goddess through understanding the stages of each aspect of her: Maiden, from infant to puberty; Mother, adult and parent; and Crone, the wise elder. The simple rituals and guided meditations will help you attain awareness and strength, while a dictionary of mythic symbols lends practical support.

Maiden, Mother, Crone is the balancing principle that has been missing from our human spiritual evolution for too long. Now is the time to look inward for completeness, for it is here we find reconnection with the Goddess, ourselves, and all of humankind.

D1297262

ABOUT THE AUTHOR

D. J. Conway was born in Hood River, Oregon, to a family of Irish-North Germanic-Native North American descent. She began her quest for knowledge of the occult more than 25 years ago, and has been involved in many aspects of New Age religion from the teachings of Yogananda to study of the Qabala, healing, herbs, and Wicca. Although an ordained minister in two New Age churches and holder of a Doctor of Divinity degree, Conway claims that her heart lies within the Pagan cultures. No longer actively lecturing and teaching as she did for years, Conway has centered her energies on writing. Several of her stories have been published in magazines, such as *Encounters*, which pertain to the field of science fantasy.

TO WRITE TO THE AUTHOR

If you wish to contact the author or would like more information about this book, please write to the author in care of Llewellyn Worldwide, and we will forward your request. Both the author and publisher appreciate hearing from you and learning of your enjoyment of this book and how it has helped you. Llewellyn Worldwide cannot guarantee that every letter written to the author can be answered, but all will be forwarded. Please write to:

D. J. Conway
c/o Llewellyn Worldwide
P.O. Box 64383-171, St. Paul, MN 55164-0383, U.S.A.

Please enclosed a self-addressed, stamped envelope or $1.00 to cover costs.
If outside the U.S.A., enclose international postal reply coupon.

MAIDEN, MOTHER, CRONE

The Myth and Reality of the Triple Goddess

D. J. Conway

2003
Llewellyn Publications
St. Paul, MN 55164-0383 U.S.A.

FIRST EDITION
Seventh Printing, 2003

Cover art: Hrana Janto
Cover design: Linda Norton
Interior art: Lisa Hunt
Book design and layout: Jessica Thoreson

Library of Congress Cataloging-in-Publication Data
Conway, D. J. (Deanna J.)
      Maiden, mother, crone: the myth and reality of the triple goddess
      / D. J. Conway.
          p.   cm.
      Includes bibliographical references and index.
      ISBN 0-87542-171-7
      1. Goddesses. 2. Trinities. 3. Goddess religion. 4. Mythology—
      Psychological aspects. I. Title.
      BL473.5.C66   1994
      291.2'114--dc20   94-6807
                                                                  CIP

Llewellyn Publications
A Division of Llewellyn Worldwide, Ltd.
P.O. Box 64383, Dept. 0-87542-171-7
St. Paul, MN 55164-0383
http://www.llewellyn.com

Printed in the United States of America

To ShadowCat,
for encouragement and friendship,

and to Jeanne,
for being my daughter.

CONTENTS

INTRODUCTION

There are a great many books on the market today relating the most plausible theories about the decline or conquest of ancient matriarchies and the rise of power of patriarchal societies, the outcome of which was suppression of women in general. This dark section of history no longer needs forceful retelling. However, the repercussions of these past actions are still with us today, strongly affecting both men and women and how they relate to each other and to everything around them. It is my hope that this book will aid the individual, whether female or male, to open new spiritual paths rather than continue on the same painful old ones of division.

Reconnection with the Great Goddess archetype and Her three faces is vital to the health of humankind on all levels. Healing the breach of distrust and inequality between the sexes is essential; peace and love must begin within the individual circle before it can be extended to the whole world and its inhabitants. For at least 2,000 years humankind has labored in its spiritual seeking without the balance of the Great Mother. She has always been there; we just have forgotten how to reach Her.

Fortunately, many of the ancient myths are still with us. These myths are like spiritual treasure maps. If we learn how to read the symbolic codes of direction, we can once more take the spiritual journey inward, through the labyrinth of the mind to the Divine Center where the Goddess patiently waits.

The Mother of all creation has no need to be thought of as the only One; She too has Her consort and companion. Every part of Her creation is brought into being and affected by the male/female, positive/negative, active/receptive, yin/yang. Her way is one of balanced living, of peaceful coexistence, of equality of sexes and races.

However, the Great Mother of all must once again have equal billing in the spiritual community; Her concepts of life must no longer be forcibly kept from humankind. The Goddess dwells within the center of our beings, deep within the collective unconscious of humankind, waiting for each of us individually to make the inward journey and ask for guidance.

Women have been learning the way back to the Goddess for some time, but it would seem some men are still struggling with the concept. Many men feel that the idea of a Goddess cannot apply directly to them. But they continue seeking for that "something" which will make them feel whole again. I hope that this book will create a spark that will help males as well as females find their way back to spiritual balance.

PART I
MYTHOLOGY:
THE SPIRITUAL MAP

I

THREE FACES OF THE GODDESS

The Great Goddess was worshipped for about 20,000 to 30,000 years of humankind's history as the prime deity, the Great Creatress. Originally the Goddess stood for unity, cooperation, and participation with all creation, while the male gods represented dissociation and separation from and dominion over Nature. After the patriarchal conquests, this idea of the Goddess changed. Eventually, Her importance in the order of things was almost forgotten entirely.

But the people continued to cling to certain ideas of Pagan spirituality. One of these was the trinity of Goddess aspects. This spiritual principle was sometimes borrowed and applied to other deities, such as the Christian Holy Trinity and the Hindu Trinity of Brahma, Vishnu, and Shiva. Over the centuries the original connotation of the trinity became buried, but the core remained.

In the twentieth century humankind began to delve deeply into worldwide mythologies. The age of advancing technology made it possible for nearly anyone who wanted to become familiar with ancient concepts of spirituality to do so. A spark ignited in thousands of men and women who felt something was missing from their spiritual lives. These pioneers began to force open the door of old knowledge and discovered behind it the Mother of all. They found Her in every culture, and in a vast majority of cultures they found Her in Her triple form. How wonderful and inexhaustible are the spiritual meanings behind the Triple Goddess! And how frustrating, for these seekers had to find the markers to Her paths by themselves. Still, the Goddess in Her triplicity was a beacon that led many to return to Her ancient ways.

Trying to understand the archetypal image of the Goddess can be the work of a lifetime. When one realizes that She is both a single archetypal entity and also a trinity of aspects, the understanding becomes more complex. Complex, but clearer in many ways and more comprehensive. For the Goddess is everything to all Her creations, and especially to both women and men. She is the beginning and ending and everything in between.

It appears from the study of mythology and ancient cultures that the characteristics of the Triple Goddess may have been first recognized in the Moon and its phases as a simple way to help humans understand an abstract entity.[1] A few cultures, such as Germany and Japan, called their Moon deities gods; the rest had Moon goddesses. The European pantheons, especially, all knew and honored the Triple Moon Goddess.

The aspects of the Triple Goddess can be compared to the main stages of human life: youth and puberty, parenthood and maturity, old age and wisdom. Many ancient cultures, as well as the modern Wiccan community, called Her by the names of Maiden, Mother, and Crone. A few had an intermediate interpretation of Goddess, God, and Divine Child. However, the designation of three female aspects was the most common and widespread.

The number three has often been a sacred number. It can still be found in folk sayings, such as good or bad luck coming in threes or a dream dreamed three times comes true. Folk tales often have three fairy godmothers, three wishes, or three (or a multiple of three) tasks to be performed. Even Shakespeare had three witches around a cauldron, an obvious but distorted picture of the Triple Goddess and Her cauldron of inspiration. Scientists say that we live in the third dimension, the physical/material world.

The Babylonians and many other ancient civilizations considered three one of their sacred and lucky numbers. It symbolized birth, life, and death; the beginning, middle, and end; childhood, adulthood, and old age; body, mind (some say soul), and spirit. The fact that the number often represented a Trinity of deities made it especially sacred.

Pythagoras[2] wrote that three is to be considered a triple Word,[3] since the Hierarchical Order must manifest itself in threes. He said that the Word expresses, conceals, and signifies. If one studies the diatonic scale discovered by Pythagoras, E above middle C is the musical note belonging to the number three. Paracelsus compared the number three to the gold in alchemy. The ancient Chinese and their philosopher Lao-Tse stated that numbers are perfect at three, for three engenders all things.

All ancient schools of inner spiritual illumination had three main steps or degrees; this can still be found in many modern organizations. The Masonic Lodges have the Apprentice, Fellowcraft, and Master. Wiccan covens have three degrees, but do not necessarily give them names or titles. The importance of three degrees or steps is a remaining fragment of ancient wisdom known to priestesses and priests. In his writings, Pythagoras alludes to this.

Numerology[4] gives various meanings for the number three, depending upon the book. In general, though, authors agree that three is a number of activity, creativity, talent, and knowledge. It is one of the triangular numbers, along with six and nine. Campbell says its color is yellow, while Heline writes that it is golden flame or illumined gold.

Why does the Goddess have three faces? If you accept the premise that humans are modeled after Her, it is easy to understand as a repeating growth cycle. If you accept that the Goddess was modeled after humans, it can be seen as an explanation of life, again a growth cycle. Personally, I find the Goddess very real, not something conjured from wish-fulfillment or imagination. When one has received very explicit directions from Her in a dream that is not a dream, one no longer questions Her reality.

The first face of the Goddess, the Maiden aspect, is the youthfulness and anticipation of life, the matrix of creation which will, when the time is ripe, produce. Whether this will be in the physical, material, mental, or spiritual depends upon the directed will of the matrix.

The Mother aspect is the culmination of the matrix set in motion to create. It is the physical desire, mental will, and spiritual love that go together to create endlessly on many levels. The mental will sets the matrix in motion; the physical desire creates its form; the spiritual love sustains it.

The Crone aspect is the most frightening to many, for the Crone represents death and dissolution. There is no way that death can be avoided, for all things have a life cycle. At the end of that cycle, things begin to malfunction and decay. We see this in everything: humans, plants, animals, stars, comets, and universes. But the Crone is not the end, for everything is recycled; nothing is wasted. Forms are changed and reformed into something else. Even science admits that nothing is destroyed; the atoms merely appear in another form.

If one accepts that the Goddess is the Great Mother, the Creatress of all, one must also accept that She is logical and cyclical in Her creations. There are always reasonable explanations, although we may not be capable of seeing them. One thing I know: there is no expendable junk in Her universe. As scientists do not know all there is to know about the workings of the universe and its many life forms, neither can we completely understand the awe-inspiring Goddess and Her universal laws. Some of the more obvious laws, such as gravity, are quickly understood. Others of a more subtle type we learn through trial and error, lifetime after lifetime.

Humans need points of reference in order to understand abstract deity qualities. The three faces of the Goddess provide that point of reference. By looking at and studying the more easily understood Triple Goddess instead of the Goddess as a whole, humans have a greater opportunity to learn about and from an intensely powerful, abstract deity personality, one existing in the spiritual realms but having influence in the physical.

II

THE IMPORTANCE OF
MYTHS

The ancient myths are primarily looked upon today as fables and legends, fantasy stories to entertain children. Until the coming of such persons as C. G. Jung, Joseph Campbell, and Mircea Eliade, myths were thought to be the literal way that ancient cultures looked at the world. Science supposedly has defined the creation and existence of the universe in more rational terms, but it has really given us more symbolic legends, explanations that we have no more way of proving or disproving than the spiritual stories behind the old myths.

Myths are, and always have been, teaching stories. They are filled with symbolic images, not necessarily of actual happenings, but more of spiritual problems, solutions, and mysteries. They were not meant to be taken literally, for they have layers of meaning that speak to all people regardless of their present state of belief or unbelief. Mythologies speak to the conscious, subconscious, and collective unconscious of all humankind, even if the myths come from unfamiliar cultures. In fact, to gain the greatest spiritual understanding one should study a wide variety of mythologies and note the similarities among them.

To understand how important symbolic language is to spiritual understanding, one must understand the divisions of the mind. The conscious mind is the state in which a person is aware of what they are seeing, hearing, tasting, etc.; it is perceiving or noticing with controlled thought and observation. The conscious mind is accessible on demand. The subconscious mind is the state that perceives or notices without a person's being aware of what they are noticing; intuition and hunches come from this area. Information exists in the subconscious mind but is not immediately available upon demand. The collective unconscious exists in the deepest areas of the mind; the information there is not readily available without training on how to access it. It is a collection of everything seen, heard, and known, not only by the individual but by every human who has ever lived.

Basic themes are repeated in mythology after mythology around the world. Similar stories appear in widely separated cultures. Their appearance may be somewhat different under various cultural guises, but a great many of the symbolic explanations are virtually the same. This fact points to a vast pool of energy and knowledge that is beyond humankind's understanding in more than a basic way. This collection of energy and knowledge has always been referred to as the gods and goddesses. C. G. Jung said that we have access to this pool of knowledge through the collective unconscious, which connects all humans.

Myths are maps that lead to spiritual understanding of humankind's position in the universe, and the relationship of humankind to the powers we call gods and goddesses. These stories also hold clues to understanding ourselves.

The symbolism of myths bridges the connection between the right and left hemispheres of the brain, speaking directly to the subconscious mind. One can see why myths are used when one realizes that the subconscious mind understands only symbols and pictures, not words. The subconscious is directly connected with the right brain, that marvelous hemisphere of creative power with the ability to create and accomplish anything it thinks is important. Using the right brain is the only way to make contact with the powers of foreseeing, healing, spiritual insight, and other psychic talents. The path from the right brain through the subconscious is the only way to reach the collective unconscious,[1] that unlimited collection of all knowledge and primal energy, a direct link with the gods and goddesses.

When the myths are read and studied, the subconscious mind absorbs the symbols and the collective unconscious[2] relates to them, even though the person on a conscious level sees nothing more than an entertaining story. This unconscious absorbtion of knowledge may be one reason why a great many mythologies were not lost through direct intent or forgetfulness.

Tenaciously the people clung to them, not fully understanding why, but telling themselves they valued them as part of their national or racial heritage. Telling the myths helped pass the time during the winter cold when life was hard. The country people, the Pagans and Heathens, held on the longest, passing the stories into "folklore" where they were eventually looked upon as fairy tales. When the last of the trained Pagan priests and priestesses died, the religious symbolism of the myths was forgotten.

It was a sad day in human history when we forgot the hidden spiritual keys and discarded the myths as nothing more than fanciful tales. And it is of great personal importance that we rediscover and re-examine these spiritual maps, the myths. For the myths hold the vital keys to our individual spiritual, mental, and physical well-being. Each person can study the myths in his or her own way, at his or her own speed, and gain important knowledge from them.

Mircea Eliade[3] writes that characters in myths can be used as examples for humans to emulate for self-improvement. It is true that one can see others acting much like Venus or Mars or even Thorr.[4] Even though most people do not believe in the old gods, you can find many of the deities' characteristics in any person walking down the street, indeed in yourself. Modeling, whether conscious, subconscious, or an emanation from the collective unconscious, appears to be a human trait. Unfortunately, some people model themselves after the less positive deities.

Suppression of the Great Goddess has created more subtle harm than undesirable character modeling. The end result of the denial of the Goddess has harmed and hindered men and women for centuries. When men denied the Goddess in women, they cut themselves off from the Primary Source, the Great Mother. Many of them lost the valuable traits of compassion and true unselfish loving. These actions in turn brought undesirable changes in women.

This unfortunate attitude toward the Goddess created many of our present world problems of imbalance and disharmony. Both women and men need to acknowledge the Great Goddess if we are to experience happy, fulfilled, and balanced physical and spiritual lives.

Mythologies hold the key to real spiritual treasures and positive growth of character, our hope for future generations. Mythologies are maps for the inward journey necessary to find that treasure—the treasure of who we are, why we are here, and where we are going, the treasure that lies deep within our own being. Without a spiritual search, the inner voice, or the voice of the Goddess, cannot be heard. Without a spiritual search, we cannot hope to make permanent positive changes in our outer life, both physically and mentally. Without individual spiritual searches, I see no way to bring inward peace to individuals or outward peace to the world.

Like Her symbol the circle, the Goddess has passed through the cycle of reverence to degradation and back to reverence. This is once more Her time in the lives of Her children. Her re-emergence will continue. Despite some objections, the Goddess is here to stay. Her very presence is causing us to question outdated ways, laws, and methods. Like the serene, all-knowing Creatress She is, the Goddess stands ready to lead us to the peace, contentment, and spiritual wisdom left untapped for centuries.

She calls us all, both women and men. She calls us, not as groups or nations or races, but as individuals. For it is only on the individual level, the personal seeking, that changes can be made and truths revealed. To make changes, we must each begin by remolding our individual lives. When enough individuals change, the ripples go out to alter communities, then nations, and finally the world. We may not see the desired changes in our generation, but they will come.

The Goddess will no longer be deterred in Her plans to return balance to the world and Her creations. Like any mother, the Great Mother feels sorrow when Her children are in pain or suffering. Her gentle voice, guiding us from the depths of our minds, calls us to new spiritual paths. And only on the spiritual paths to Oneness and balance can we begin to heal. We need no longer say the Goddess is coming. She is here!

III

IN THE BEGINNING

In the beginning, the Goddess was known, loved, and revered by humankind. There are no pictorial representations of male gods among the earliest cultures, except for those in the role of son or lover. The Goddess, as the Creatress, was given primary reverence.

Archaeology has turned up many clues that point to the earliest cultures being matriarchies; this does not mean female-controlled, but rather ruling partnerships between men and women. Because the women were responsible for bearing and raising the all-important children, they tended to live in fixed groups, agricultural communities that provided a stable base for the hunting groups of males. Women domesticated animals, learned the intricacies of growing plants, and established small religious centers. They developed medicine, divination, writing, pottery, weaving, and other types of art and domestic crafts. The female elders passed the laws that regulated the communities, keeping the people in peaceful harmony among themselves and with outsiders.

Archaeology's present methods at dating antiquities are still being refined; knowledge is limited. As new methods of dating are discovered, the time of humankind on this planet is pushed further and further into the past. At present calculations, matriarchies and worship of the Goddess extend back 20,000 to 30,000 BCE.[1] During Paleolithic times, sacred objects and the dead were painted with red ocher, a symbol of menstrual blood for re-creation. Religious sites such as caves and temples contain the remnants of shells, particularly cowrie shells which represent female sexual organs. Ancient cave paintings, bas-reliefs, and statues were overwhelmingly of the Goddess; male depictions during these times were only in peripheral positions, as were their symbols.

Somewhat later in history, the Goddess began to be pictured with animals, trees, and symbols of water. Sometimes She was portrayed as being part animal. This was a symbolic linkage of Her direct connection with all Nature.

One example of how male archaeologists refused to deal with Goddess symbols is shown by some ancient paintings depicting figures holding what were interpreted as spears with backward-pointing barbs. These were called portrayals of hunting males. Upon closer examination by women in the field, it was discovered that these "spears" were branches or plants.[2] The stylized painted figures were really holding branches as part of religious rituals, much as the later Hebrews used palm branches. One of the primary reasons for

An Early Goddess Representation

this misinterpretation by early male archaeologists was that the Goddess just did not fit into preconceived ideas.

All these depictions of the Goddess point to an abstract realization by ancient peoples—that the Great Mother was the source and regeneratrix of all life forms. One can still find that meaning in the descriptions of various goddesses. Examples of this are Magna Mater, Ishtar, Astarte, and Lilith of the Middle East; Bona Dea, Atargatis, Ceres, and Cybele of Rome; Isis, Nut, and Maat of Egypt; Demeter, Kore, and Hera in Greece.

Some of the richest sites of Neolithic Goddess culture and matriarchies have been found in Anatolia, Turkey. Among these sites are the ruined cities of Catal Huyuk and Hacilar, dating back as far as 6,500 BCE. Archaeologists have discovered an abundance of red ocher burials, collections of fossils and shells, and innumerable little Goddess statues. In fact, these Goddess statues have been found from the Middle East to India, and even in many European sites. Although these Turkish sites have only been excavated back as far as 6,500 BCE, they show a remarkably advanced religion and civilization complete with symbology and mythology.

It is known that by 6,000 BCE agricultural societies were expanding rapidly throughout the Mesopotamian area and into southeastern Europe. The islands of Crete and Cyprus were settled by sea wanderers from the Turkish civilizations. Under these matriarchies there was equality between the sexes, and a vast expansion of arts, crafts, and writing.

As far back as 7,000 years ago Goddess cultures in certain sections of Europe were flourishing. These matriarchies spread north from the Aegean and Adriatic Seas into Czechoslovakia, southern Poland, and the western part of the Ukraine. They practiced extensive agriculture and animal husbandry (although they did not train horses). Advanced work was done in pottery and stone work. Even copper metallurgy was practiced by 5,500 BCE in south-central Europe. Sailing boats were used beginning in about the sixth millennia.

Sometime between 7,000 and 3,500 BCE, Europeans began to develop complex cultural societies that included specialization in crafts and religious and governmental organizations. They used copper and gold for both religious objects and personal jewelry. A simple script for recording was introduced. Equal burial rites were performed for both sexes, as seen by grave excavations.

The greatest difference between the matriarchies and later patriarchal cultures is shown by the lack of extensive warfare under Goddess-guided civilizations. Early matriarchal cities were not built on high, steep places; there were no enormous stone walls or hill forts. In Catal Huyuk and Hacilar, for example, there is absolutely no evidence of warfare for over 1,500 years.

In the ruins of these early peaceful matriarchies, temple remains with their vivid paintings show that priestesses and women's arts and crafts were held sacred. It is possible that the arts were first practiced within the religious arenas and considered gifts from the Goddess.[3] Female figures and symbols continued to occupy a central place of importance in European and Middle Eastern arts until the takeover by male-dominated groups.

Then a time of great change descended upon the matriarchies. Female cultures were swallowed up and reformed under male-dominated groups. The mythologies speak only of hordes of patriarchal warriors sweeping into area after area. It was rare that any matriarchal culture could withstand this armed aggression. The only exceptions were the Amazons, who fought their way out of such a situation and, thereafter, lived in exclusive female-only groups, dealing with men only for reproductive purposes. The Amazons became such effective, fierce warriors that even the Greeks grudgingly admired them. The women of the Celtic and Norse races also were known for their fierceness and their ability to use weapons, although they did not segregate themselves from men as did the Amazons.

After conquering the matriarchies, the new patriarchal rulers seem to have made no violent attempts to root out the concept of the Goddess. In fact, there is no evidence that most of these men really tried to do this. The most they did was rearrange and rewrite some of the myths.

Some of the mythologies left intact the creation stories surrounding the Primary Source, the Great Goddess, who created Herself out of chaos and then by Herself formed the universe. Others were rewritten to present male creators. Still others kept the old Goddess myths and added, side by side, the new stories. The majority rewrote the tale of creation of the world's creatures, plants, and humankind to include a co-creator, Her son/lover. This points to a strong possibility that men too were aware of the importance of the Goddess.

At this point in cultural mythologies, major changes were made. The Great Goddess became the wife of the major God. Other aspects or goddesses became sisters, wives, and mistresses of various other gods. A few goddesses escaped this pairing as there was no way, logically or illogically, that they would fit into this classification.

A good example of a rewritten creation story comes from Assyro-Babylonian mythology. Everything began with Apsu, the sweet waters that produce springs and rivers, and Tiamat, the sea or salty waters. They combined their forces to create the universe and the gods. Tiamat was the Great Goddess, who alone held the tablets of supreme wisdom. But Apsu, consort of Tiamat, plotted against the god-children because he did not like their troublesome behavior; the god Ea destroyed him. Tiamat, who had not supported the destruction of Her children, then fought against them. Choosing a second consort, Kingu, Tiamat gave birth to hundreds of monsters to help Her. All the original gods were afraid to confront their mother in war until Marduk, son of Ea, went against her, with the understanding that he would be king of the gods if he won. After fierce fighting, Marduk won. He cut Tiamat's body in two, making the sky from one part and the Earth from the other. Then he chained the monsters in the underworld and made humans out of Kingu's blood. The tablets of wisdom he kept for himself.

It is quite easy in this myth to extrapolate what probably occasioned the revision of a Goddess tale. In the distant past there was a peaceful Goddess-oriented culture that allowed other religious ideas to flourish. The priestesses and priests of this culture held the keys to spiritual knowledge. Following the Goddess's injunction of peace and individuality, the

Tiamat

culture did not react in violence to the rumors of discontent among those who believed in other deities. A leader of a God religion arose who became strong enough to replace the Goddess with another deity. This priestly leader took the books or tablets of spiritual mystery-wisdom from the temple of the Goddess, thus transferring the main worship from Tiamat to Marduk.

My interpretation is given only to show how one can look for small buried truths and clues within old myths and interpret them on a physical level. Spiritual interpretations are much more complex.

Whether or not humankind as a whole believes in the Goddess, She exists. You can call Her an archetype, a force of Nature, or a symbol, it matters not. She can, and does, manifest Herself differently to each human. We need to return to the fact that the Goddess's face can be seen in all Her creations. Her powers remain as awesome and far-reaching as in the beginning. She has never made an injunction that humans must suffer and practice unreasonable denials to please Her; she only requires that we move in Her cycles of being, at one with each other, the seasons, and the planet.

The Goddess may be seen as ruling over the world in one sense, but in a larger interpretation She is the world. She can be understood spiritually by every individual because She is manifest in each of us.[4] Because She is manifest in each person, She does not sanction dominion of one sex or race. Her aspects slip constantly from one form and face into another, for rigidity is foreign to Her laws.[5]

The Goddess archetype is at the core of every human's essential being, as the physical mother is the center of every small child's life. The Goddess is not found by searching aimlessly through the world. The Goddess can only be discovered by going within, by searching the subconscious and collective unconscious for the symbols that mark the path leading to Her. If we do not search for and find Her, we will continue to feel incomplete.

THE IMPORTANCE OF RECONNECTION

Reconnecting with the Goddess is not just a woman-experience but a human-experience, greatly needed for the well-being and positive development of our species. Acknowledging and reforming the link with the

Mother of all is vital to all levels of human growth. Spiritually, acknowledgement of Her three aspects and their practical application in human lives can create a foundation for ourselves and future generations.

According to C. G. Jung, we have always known everything because of the collective unconscious accessible to every human. Each one of us has the possibility for the deepest insight into the most complex aspects of the Goddess's being and the laws of Her universe, but we have forgotten how to access that information. Study of mythological symbols will help us relearn the way to the Divine Center. The Divine Feminine is required for healthy physical, mental, emotional, and spiritual lives. To understand Her we must understand Her three faces or aspects, for they are a mirror of our own lives. They are the first clues to changing ourselves.

When we speak of acknowledgement of the Goddess and return to Her laws, we are not suggesting an overthrow of other religions. There will always be humans who feel a burning desire and close tie with those systems of spiritual thought. One of the fascinating traits of the Great Mother is diversity, and this includes all areas of life and religion. Everything and everyone has a place in Her system of cycles, Her rules of checks and balances.

The Triple Goddess, the three faces of human life, are ingrained in the human subconscious and collective unconscious. A change of direction of spiritual thought, a return and incorporation of the Goddess in our lives, will create a ripple effect in all levels of existence, especially the spiritual health of all humankind. This is not an impossible journey to make, for the Goddess teaches tolerance, peace, love, and respect. Each person, regardless of sex, race, or religion, has important, valuable contributions to make. By changing ourselves, inwardly and outwardly, we take the first step toward changing the world into a better place for all to live.

PART II
THE MAIDEN

IV

THE GODDESS AS MAIDEN

The first aspect of the Goddess is the Maiden, sometimes called the Virgin or Huntress. She is spring, the fresh beginning of all things. The Maiden is the continuation of all life, the repeating of endless cycles of birth and rebirth, both of the body and of the spirit. She is the dawn, eternal youth and vigor, enchantment and seduction, the waxing Moon. Traditionally, Her color is white, denoting innocence and newness.

Although the Maiden is most often associated with youth and puberty, Her attributes can be experienced by anyone, male or female, in any stage of life. We cannot reverse the actual aging process of the body however much we submit ourselves to body tucks and wrinkle creams and diets. But within the mind, we have the unique ability to experience all three aspects of the Goddess whenever we choose. Indeed, it is beneficial to our mental, emotional, and spiritual health if we periodically refresh ourselves in this manner. And when we improve these areas of our lives, our physical health improves also. Too often we lock ourselves into one phase, thereby missing the growth and experience of the other two. By studying and meditating upon the Threefold Goddess, it is possible to bring life back into balance, back to the rhythm of Nature, back to sanity and wholeness.

Through the Maiden aspect of the Goddess we learn to see the beauty of all things; the wonder of Nature at work in all creation. The Maiden is the budding strength of natural and Nature magick at work everywhere. This aspect is the mental ability to find delight in a butterfly winding its way through a patch of sunlight; the slow rise and fall of waves on a beach of brilliant sand. Even the contemplation of a trickle of raindrops down a window can be a means of flexing mental muscles long out of use.

The Maiden face of the Goddess can be valuable when we need a fresh perspective on things—when we have reached a point in our lives when we feel directionless and do not have a clue as to what to do or where to go next. She can be the Creatress of new ideas and new beginnings.

But as the other phases of the Goddess subtly blend into each other, so does the Maiden blend with areas of the Mother and the Crone, completing the cycle of the Threefold Goddess. The Maiden has attributes that can seem frightening, as in Her form as the Huntress and Mistress of the Woodlands. Even as the Huntress, though, senseless destruction is abhorrent to Her. She is the armed keeper of the Mother's universal laws, a swift messenger from the Divine Source of life. She can deal out punishment to offenders of those laws, not blindly as with the figure of blindfolded Justice, but dispassionately as a guardian of balance.

The Maiden is a friend and companion of all young creatures, more a comrade than nurturer, as is the Mother phase. She is free with Her feelings and emotions, often expressing Herself in sudden decisions. She is aware of Her sexuality, sometimes holding it at bay, other times abandoning all else to revel in it. The term Virgin does not mean physical virginity, that state so strangely and highly prized by patriarchal males; this "virgin" means independent, Her own person. No one rules Her. She is responsible for Her own actions, in adherence with the Mother's laws. She knows who She is and dreams of the potential for what She can become.

The Maiden can make Herself felt mentally without warning and when least expected. Her shyness and coyness may arise in sexual partners at any time of life when a renewal is experienced in their relationship. Her wonder and reverence of life may surface when a new child or grandchild is held for the first time. The sudden awareness of a sunset or a scene in Nature may trigger deep spiritual feelings that make one feel renewed and truly part of all creation.

The Maiden aspect of the Goddess is synonymous with the physical stage of puberty in humans. In females, She represents the waxing Moon of beginning menstruation. But to both sexes She symbolizes the mixed feelings of approaching adulthood and the stirrings of the sexual drive. She is shyness and assertiveness, confidence and fear, all rolled into one. Understanding the Maiden will help humans understand themselves. If one is past this stage She can still help, for the Maiden can unearth long buried reasons, however remote, for certain youthful actions and help one be tolerant with oneself.

The Maiden is known in many forms and variations around the world. She is an essential part of the cycle, of the Threefold Goddess, yet She is unique in Herself. Her empathy for all creatures, Her curiosity about all things, Her determination to be Her individual self and all She is capable of achieving—these are qualities that are vital to human happiness and development. The Maiden shows us the way, the clues to safely passing through the spiritual labyrinth to the calm center. Teasing with laughter and promises, She runs before us, enticing us to follow the path we fear the most, the labyrinth deep within our minds that leads to the deeply buried collective unconscious. There lies the treasure, the true source of all knowledge and ideas. The Maiden is the Way-Shower, the Keeper of the Keys, the seed stage of creation, whether that creation be physical, mental, or spiritual. Without Her aid we have little chance of making a safe journey or finding the treasure at all.

THE MAIDEN AND MAGICK

Calling upon the goddesses who represent the Maiden aspect of the Great Goddess can be useful in various types of magick, even simple candle-burning. Any type of new beginning is in the domain of the Maiden. Spring is the Maiden's part of the year, the waxing Moon Her monthly time of power. Pagan holiday festivals connected with the Maiden are Imbolc on February 1 and the Spring Equinox. The Winter Solstice She shares with the Mother and the Crone. Christianity kept this celebration of the Spring Equinox as Easter.

Using the Maiden, magick can involve any meditation, motivated ritual, candleburning, or seed or bulb planting (which can be a type of ritual). Her power affects anything from working for success in a new job to welcoming a new baby into the family. There are powerful creative forces available for magick in the Maiden aspect.

Examples of the type of rituals using the Maiden's power follow:

1. Any new beginning, or even the hopes and plans for new beginnings.
2. When taking on a new job, or planning to apply for a new job.
3. During the first steps of new ideas, whatever they are.
4. Whenever you plan or begin a complete turnaround in your life.
5. Whenever you begin any new phase in your life.
6. On moving into a new house or apartment.
7. On entering a new school or going back to school after a delay in education.
8. Any journey that is connected with anticipated changes. This can be anything from a trip to visit family to a vacation to give one a new perspective on life.
9. The beginning of a new relationship, love, or friendship.
10. Plans for getting pregnant.
11. The birth of a child.
12. The first menstruation for girls.
13. Puberty on reaching the teens for boys.

A pastel candle, the color chosen to compliment the action you wish to occur, can be used in a candleburning ritual. While holding the candle, carefully think of what you wish to happen, mentally infusing the candle with your desires. Be certain that your plans do not entail controlling someone else or causing them harm. Then light the candle and leave it in a safe place to burn out.

Other ways to symbolize the power of new beginnings and happenings are to plant seeds, bulbs, or new plants. As you care for these growing creations, you make yourself repeatedly aware of the growth and expansion of the request you placed before the Maiden.

The use of the Maiden's power does not depend upon your actual belief in a Goddess. You may see this aspect of the Divine Feminine as a subconscious and collective unconscious archetype that has nothing to do with a deity. If one believes in the tremendous untapped power of the subconscious mind, one can see clearly how the use of this energy is unaffected by the belief in a particular deity.

If, however, one does believe in the Goddess as deity and has felt even the fringes of Her awesome power, then practice has shown that the manifestation of desires is more likely to be full and true. Perhaps this is because there is no doubt in the mind of the person calling upon this power. Perhaps, though, there is a greater reason for this success ratio: the Goddess in all Her aspects resides on another plane of existence and will help those who learn how to reach and call upon Her.

V

WORLD MAIDEN
MYTHS

The Maiden aspect of the Great Goddess is known and can be seen in many ancient pantheons around the world. There are a few cultures, however, where the Maiden was not known at all.

Perhaps the best known examples of the Maiden aspect are found in ancient Greece, where the metaphorical story of Demeter and Kore was told for centuries. Archaeological evidence points to the very sound premise that Demeter and Kore, and other goddesses, came from the matriarchal civilization of Crete; Crete, in turn, received these deities from more ancient matriarchies when it was settled by people from ancient Turkey.

The Homeric hymns, in particular the Hymn of Demeter, relate the complete tale of Kore (whose name literally means "the Maiden") and Her mother Demeter.[1] Charlene Spretnak[2] gives what she considers to be a truer matriarchal rendition of the Kore story; it is probable that she is correct since all goddess myths were changed in some manner when patriarchy took over.

In the myth of Cretan origin, Spretnak says that Demeter, the Grain Mother, gave humans the gift of agriculture and civilization. Her beautiful daughter Persephone, also called Kore the Maiden, helped Her to watch over the growing grain. The girl liked to wander the hills after the grain was growing to be among the wildflowers, especially gathering red poppies.

One day Kore-Persephone told Demeter that She had met the spirits of the dead drifting aimlessly over the Earth, hovering about their old homes and families. "They seemed lost," the girl said. "Do they not have anyone to watch over them in the underworld?"

Demeter answered that She was also mistress of the underworld as well as of the growing grain. Her most important function was caring for the crops, and She could not take the time to care for the spirits of the dead.

"Then I will go and care for them," Kore-Persephone said. Demeter tried to dissuade the girl, but She was determined. The girl gathered red poppies and sheaves of grain to take with Her in remembrance of Her mother's upper domain. Demeter led Her to a deep chasm that went far down into the Earth. The Grain Mother handed Her daughter a torch to light Her way, kissed Her, and wept as the girl disappeared into the chilly abyss.

Kore-Persephone walked downward in the cold darkness until She came to an enormous cavern filled with the spirits of the dead. There the girl set up the torch near a rocky throne; beside it She placed a dish of pomegranate seeds, food of the dead. She called each spirit to Her, embraced it, and marked its forehead with pomegranate juice. This initiation marked a preparation for rebirth into the upper world.

Meantime, Demeter continued to mourn for Her daughter. The crops stopped growing; everything became dormant, the weather cold. After several months, Demeter noticed a crocus blooming. She knew Kore-Persephone was returning to Her. The Grain Mother waved Her hands in blessing over the land, and the crops flourished. Animals began to bear young again. Soon Kore-Persephone emerged from the cleft in the Earth and greeted Her mother with joy. But part of each year the young Maiden returns to the underworld to comfort and guide the spirits of the dead. While She is gone, Her mother weeps and awaits Her daughter's return in the spring.

It is obvious in this rendition by Spretnak that the Goddess and Her Maiden daughter are unpolluted by later changes. Demeter is the Mother aspect of the Goddess, the energy of grain and life after it has been planted. But Kore-Persephone is a more complex version of the Goddess; it is also possible that She is an older-definition of Demeter, a facet

Kore-Persephone

grafted onto a later, more inclusive form. Kore-Persephone is both the virginal Maiden, independent of the Earthly responsibilities of Her mother, yet also an image of the Crone, the death-life Goddess of rebirth.

The later Homeric hymns give a different version of the same story. Demeter is still the Grain Mother, with Kore Her beautiful daughter. However, Zeus, ruler of gods and men, secretly promised the girl to his brother Hades. Kore wandered over the hills picking wildflowers when She saw a narcissus. As She stooped to pick it, the ground opened and She was swallowed up by the Earth. Hades, Lord of the dead, raped Her as She fell into his domain.

Frantic with worry, Demeter searched everywhere. Finally, the Goddess Hecate told Demeter that She heard the girl's screams as She was raped. Together, the Goddesses went to ask Helios, the Sun god, who saw everything from his chariot. He told them of Zeus's bargain and that Hades had the girl locked up in his underworld kingdom.

Demeter was furious. Her pleas to Zeus for Her daughter's return fell on deaf ears. Full of anger and sorrow, Demeter withdrew Her vital energy from the Earth and began wandering aimlessly among humans in the disguise of an old woman. Eventually, the Goddess came to the city of Eleusis where Celeos, the daughter of the king, and Metaneira, queen, took Her in to care for the royal child Demophoon.

Demeter decided to make the child immortal and each night passed him through flame. The queen saw this and in horror stopped the proceedings. The Goddess revealed Herself to the queen and asked that the city of Eleusis erect a temple to Her. Then She taught Metaneira the secret, sacred rites that later became so famous, the Eleusinian Mysteries.

All this time the Earth had failed to produce anything, and Zeus knew he must make amends. In turn he sent each of the gods and goddesses to Demeter to entreat Her to release Her growing energies, but She refused. "Not until I am reunited with My daughter," She answered.

At last Zeus sent Hermes to the underworld to get Kore, now known as Persephone, queen of the land of the dead. Hades, reluctant to give up his new queen, tricked the girl into eating a pomegranate seed before She left with the heavenly messenger.

Demeter was overjoyed at Her daughter's return. When the Goddess learned that Kore-Persephone had eaten the pomegranate seed, She knew She must share Her daughter part of each year with Hades. So each autumn Demeter's sorrow begins; the Earth loses its growing energies and lies dormant through the winter months. When the spring comes and

Persephone returns from the land of the dead, Demeter once more waves Her hands in blessing over the Earth, and it and its creatures are renewed.

The rape of Kore-Persephone is a vital clue that this myth was changed by a patriarchal society. But evidently the conquering tribes felt no need to stamp out the older goddesses. This is an enormous difference from the Cretan story of the young Maiden who willingly went to the underworld to prepare spirits for rebirth.

Both myths have a number of similar spiritual themes that are still important today. True understanding and compassion can only be fully experienced after letting go of what we often think of as the safe and accepted way of thinking. Opening oneself to the influx of new and different ideas arising from the collective unconscious can be an unsettling experience, but necessary if one is to expand spiritually. When we attempt the journey inward, at first we find ourselves in a frightening place, a seemingly dark cavern, an abyss, often filled with the ghosts of our past. All the memories of past actions, positive and negative, surround us, begging for recognition, our blessing, and release.

The only way to change the negative memories into positive energy is to forgive yourself and any others involved, then find one good thing that came from the situation. If one looks hard enough, at least one positive result can be found. This releases the memory and its painful after-effects that linger like a thorn in the subconscious. No memory can ever be totally erased; once something has occurred it cannot be undone, but its pain can be lessened. The negative energy you regenerate by reviewing your old thoughts of regret, anger, and fear now can be channeled into positive energy.

Kore-Persephone made the terrifying journey downward by Herself; Demeter could not accompany Her daughter. Each of us must make the journey through the labyrinth of our minds alone, our only companions being our thoughts and memories, the ghosts of things long dead. But we have a map, the knowledge found in old spiritual myths; and a torch, the enlightenment of the Maiden who rises from the depths of the collective unconscious to guide us.

The ancient Eleusinian Mysteries symbolized in mystic rites Kore-Persephone's journey into the abyss and back again. The deeper part of these spiritual rituals were difficult and not for everyone; not every person can face the journey through the labyrinth to stand, all defects exposed, before the Divine Center. The Mysteries, open to both men and women,[3] were bound by oaths of secrecy; they were such an intense spiritual experience that many of Greece's highly educated thinkers were initiates.[4]

Another goddess who falls into the category of the Maiden was Hestia (Greek), or Vesta (Roman). She was the elder sister of Zeus (Jupiter), the oldest of the Olympians, and remained a physical virgin. In Greece She had no temples, but the Temple of Vesta, manned by the Vestal Virgins, was an important part of the Roman scene.[5] No house or temple was considered sanctified until Hestia entered in the form of the hearth flame. She is seldom mentioned in the myths, but when mention is made, the goddess is spoken of with love, respect, and awe.[6] Pythagoras called Her fire the center of the Earth.[7]

Hestia/Vesta was the keeper of the flame of the domestic hearth[8] and the ceremonial fire, the "one of Light," a gentle and reserved deity. She represents the chaste fire of divinity that burns deep within each person, that spark of the Goddess that makes us a fragment of the Supreme Creatress Herself. Hestia never required any blood sacrifices; purity of soul was a greater gift.

The Greek Artemis was a Moon goddess and Virgin Huntress whose worship was brought from the Middle East, probably originating in a matriarchy.[9] The Greeks also called Her the Huntress of Souls[10] and a shape-shifter. She was the protectress of wild places and wild animals; Artemis knows the deep places in Nature where one can rest and regain strength. It was said She was quick to protect and rescue those who appealed to Her for help, particularly women who were harassed or threatened by men. Violence for its own sake was abhorrent to Her, yet She was swift to deal out punishment to offenders. Strangely enough, although this goddess was Virgin and Her priestesses did not consort with men, She was the protectress of women during childbirth and loved singing and dancing. Callisto was one of Artemis's titles used to denote Her connections with the bear, one of Her sacred creatures. *Artemisia absinthium*, or the herb wormwood, was named after Her.[11]

One myth about Artemis relates the story of Actaeon[12] coming upon the goddess while She was bathing with Her nymphs. Instead of turning away, he crept closer and was discovered spying. Artemis changed him into a stag, which Her hounds (the Alani) tore to pieces.[13]

Spiritually, this implies that one must be prepared mentally and emotionally for the journey through the labyrinth. One cannot, or rather should not, try to force one's way into spiritual mysteries for which one is not ready. When the seeker is spiritually prepared, the Maiden invites. Then, and only then, are the mysteries revealed in all their intricacies and beauty. Seeking through spiritual mysteries so as to gain power and prestige eventually backlashes, almost without exception, upon the abuser.

The animal passions and mentality (stag) take control. Our own subconscious judgement (the Maiden's hounds) will create learning-punishment circumstances whether we consciously believe we are wrong or not.

The Roman version of this goddess, named Diana, was very similar.[14] She was called the Lunar Virgin;[15] Her festivals were May 26-31 and August 13 and 15. Twin sister of Apollo, this goddess was a feminine balance to Her brother.[16] Like Artemis, Diana was called Many-Breasted, symbolizing Her creating and nourishing all creatures. Britomartis or Dictynna[17] was an ancient Cretan virgin forest huntress and may well have been the original form of Artemis/Diana.[18] Fauna,[19] a Roman goddess of wild creatures, was another form of Diana.

Athene (Greek), or Minerva[20] (Roman), a Holy Virgin and Maiden goddess, was the deity of wisdom, civilization, the arts, peace, and justice. Although She was most commonly portrayed armored, She disliked senseless violence. She was not above defending Herself, though, as seen in the story of the attack upon Her by Ares; the goddess laid him out with a huge boundary stone. Especially sacred to Her were the owl,[21] oak, and intertwined snakes. She was absolutely chaste and gave Her aid only to those She thought deserving. One of Her titles, Athene Parthenia, gave Her name to both the city of Athens and the Parthenon (Virgin-temple) there. Athene was called the goddess of women's rights and freedom, protector of the arts and cities. Tradition says She taught humans how to break and breed horses.

A much more ancient image of Athene shows the goddess as an awesome female figure with snakes wound around Her head and edging Her robe. This snake motif (the Great Goddess's gift of the kundalini renewing power to humans) was shown on later statues as the head of the Gorgon[22] on Athene's shield. Sometimes a blend of Virgin-Crone, Athene was considered a death goddess when She displayed this shield.

One interpretation of the story of Her birth may symbolize the inability of the conquering patriarchal society to subdue Athene's importance and power. She was a very ancient matriarchal goddess worshipped long before these new clans came. The myth says that a prophecy was given to Zeus, Her father, when Metis (Wisdom), Her mother, was pregnant: the child would be more powerful than Zeus. So Zeus swallowed the pregnant Metis, thinking that the unborn child would never be born to challenge him. After a time, though, the sky god began to suffer a terrible headache, so bad that he begged Hephaestus to split open his head. Out sprang Athene, fully grown, fully armed, and shaking a javelin.

True wisdom cannot be suppressed or conquered. When a person starts down a spiritual path, he or she must learn to acknowledge and accept the wisdom gained through the inward journey. Once spiritual wisdom (prophecy) is learned, it cannot be unlearned (swallowed). Everything we learn or do is recorded forever in the subconscious mind. Sooner or later any suppressed spiritual knowledge will force its way to the front, fully grown and demanding our attention. It may even cause us a few problems (headache) until we do something positive about it.

Another goddess of the Maiden aspect was Hebe, the youngest daughter of Zeus and Hera. Among the Romans She was called Juventas. She was goddess of the dawn and the East, youth, and the cupbearer to Her father until replaced by the boy Ganymede.[23] In later tales, She was married to the hero Herakles after he was taken up to Olympus.[24] In the town of Phlius, in Argolis, there was a temple to Her where freed slaves hung up their chains in Her honor. Hebe was a personal servant of Her mother Hera, helping Hera to yoke Her chariot.

The East was considered by many cultures to be the place of rebirth, whether physically or metaphorically. When we have reached the Divine Center in our spiritual journey, we are refreshed from the cup (cauldron); the Maiden is the Mother's messenger and helper in this. Renewed through this experience, we are able to free ourselves from slavery to the physical and material (chains). With the Maiden's wisdom, we become masters of the physical (chariot).

The Romans also adopted a Libyan Virgin goddess called Astraea, "Starry One." Her symbols were the judgement scales and the zodiac sign of Libra. Like Maat, She dealt with the fates of humans.

The Egyptian goddess Maat[25] expresses another important facet of the Maiden: the sense of impartial, divine justice. As truth, Maat stood between illusion and reality, good and evil. It was said that when Maat received no honor, chaos reigned. In the beginning, She arose from the primal waters of the abyss with Ra, thus She was self-created. Although the goddess was not paired with Ra, She represents the positive/negative role needed for creation. The Egyptians called Her the "light of the world," saying She ruled over heaven, Earth, and the underworld.[26]

At death it was believed that every soul was weighed against Maat; in some tomb murals only Her ostrich plume[27] is shown on the scales. She was associated with the heart (moral judgements) and held the ankh, the life symbol. The All-Seeing Eye was Her symbol long before it was transferred to the god Horus.

Maat's symbol of the ostrich plume may suggest a connection with the creation story of the Cosmic Egg. In predynastic burials, discs of ostrich eggshell have been found.[28] Her "justice" went beyond physical laws into the realm of sincerity and universal order.[29]

When one journeys inward toward the Divine Center, one must see past self-illusion to the reality of the truth. Nothing positive can emerge unless the absolute truth of being and life is recognized. All lies and self-delusions must be stripped away; the truth of actions must be seen clearly, or chaos alone will reign in the physical life.

Neith[30] was called by the Egyptians the Lady of the West and the Huntress. Her name actually meant "I come from myself," or self-begotten; the Greeks identified Her with Athene. Part of Her sanctuary at Sais was a school of medicine called the House of Life. A bow and two arrows were Her characteristic symbols.

Here again we find the Maiden Huntress, stalking the forests of the mind. Her arrows are both killing and healing, making us dispense with old harmful habits and accept new positive ones.

Bast

Anuket, or Anqet, The Clasper, was considered to be the source of the Nile river. Her four arms represented the union of male and female principles. E. A. Wallis Budge, a respected translator of ancient Egyptian writings, called Her The One who was self-begotten, yet a virgin when She birthed the Sun god.

The Egyptian cat goddess Bast was identified by the Greeks with Artemis or Diana, who were also called the mother of all cats.[31] Herodotus said that the great sacred shrine in Bubastis was built in Her honor. Bast represented the gentle, creating power of the Sun.[32]

The Lady of the Double Granary was Renenet, goddess of nursing babies; She gave each child its secret soul-name[33] and future fate. Sometimes She had a cobra head, but other times was a woman wearing the plumes of Maat. She stood with the personal spiritual protector when the soul was weighed and judged.

There were several goddesses among the Celtic clans that fit the Maiden aspect. Since the Celts lived both on the European continent and the Isles, their deities often had different names.

Anu, which may be a form of Danu, was considered the greatest of the Celtic goddesses in Ireland, Mother Earth. She formed a triad with Badb and Macha. As the flowering fertility goddess, fires were lit for Her at Summer Solstice. Her priestesses comforted and taught the dying, preparing them for descent into the cauldron and ascending once more in rebirth. There are hints that Her husband was Bile, similar to Hades.[34] This would seem to classify Her with Kore-Persephone. She is a mysterious goddess since little is known of Her.

Blodeuwedd, a Welsh Maiden goddess, was known as the Ninefold[35] Goddess of the Western Isles of Paradise, again a connection with death and reincarnation. Like Athene, owls were sacred to Blodeuwedd. She dealt with lunar mysteries and initiations. Myth says that She was created from blossoms of oak, broom, and meadowsweet by Gwydion and Math as a wife for the young god Lleu.[36] Her name actually means "flower-face."

In time, Blodeuwedd fell in love with the dark hunting god Gronw Pebyr of the forest and plotted to kill Her husband. Lleu told Her how he could be killed,[37] and Gronw did it. When Lleu was restored to life, Gwydion chased Blodeuwedd through the forests, finally changing Her into an owl.[38] Robert Graves quotes Blodeuwedd as saying She had nine powers;[39] this shows the blending and multiples of Maiden-Mother-Crone.

Here again, we may have evidence of a rewritten myth with the goddess Blodeuwedd coming and going in importance. Whatever hap-

Blodeuwedd

pened, Blodeuwedd's form as an owl (a Goddess symbol of wisdom) shows that She retained some of Her power and importance, though in a muted manner.

The goddess Brigit was known throughout Ireland, Wales, Spain, and France. Sometimes She was called the Triple Brigits, the Three Blessed Ladies of Britain, or the Three Mothers. The exclusive female priesthood at Her sanctuary in Kildare[40] kept an ever-burning fire; there were 19 priestesses, representing the 19-year cycle of the Celtic "Great Year." Brigit was considered a virgin deity, but Her priestesses, the *kelles*,[41] consorted with men. The Celts said She ruled over physicians and healing, divination and prophecy, smithcraft and domestic animals.

Brigit was a poetess, one of the daughters of the Dagda. However, She had another name, Breo-saighead, meaning fiery arrow or power. These attributes of healing and punishment point to the Maiden's dual role as guide and protectress through the labyrinth, but also as divine justice in making us face the reality of ourselves.

Very little is known of the Irish goddess Flidhais or Flidais, except that She rode in a chariot drawn by deer and was a shapeshifter.[42] Her domain was the forests where She ruled over woodland and wild animals.

Spiritually, Flidhais symbolizes dominion over the darkness (woodlands) and unknown qualities (wild animals) of the subconscious mind.

Even in the Arthurian romances, we find evidence of the Triple Goddess. Elaine, the Lily Maid, was the Virgin or Maiden aspect. British tradition says that the islands were settled by Trojans. Since Elaine bears the same name as Elen, the first British-Trojan queen, it is possible that the idea behind Her came from the Mediterranean area at some point in the past.

Blancheflor, also called the Lily Maid, was the White Flower of the Maiden aspect. Celtic romances say that She initiated Percivale into the fairy religion before the Christian priests converted him.

The Saxons had a Spring goddess called Eostre or Ostara.[43] She may well have been originally from India, since Beowulf spoke of the Ganges' waters being near Eostre's home.[44]

The Germanic-Nordic cultures knew of two Maiden-type goddesses: Gefion and Idunn. Although Gefion was not a physical virgin, She was the goddess who received virgins at death. Fertility of crops and land were within Her powers as was a favorable turn of events or luck.

A Swedish legend of Gefion the Giver tells how She disguised Herself as an old woman adept in magick and pleased the king Gylfi. In payment, the king told Her She could have as much land as She could mark with a plow in a day and a night. The bullocks She harnessed were Her four shape-shifting Giant sons. She drove in the plowshare and detached a huge section of Earth which She dragged into the sea; this became known as the island of Seeland.[45]

The conscious mind is often impressed and pleased with the results of magick.[46] It will allow us to accept the ideas of magick and the old gods because the physical is gaining something. It generously allows us to take what we want, to practice magick and worship in ancient ways, to delve into deeper areas, like the plow cutting into the Earth. Then it realizes too late that we have created a safe spiritual sanctuary (island) within the Mother (sea) and there is nothing it can do about our new spiritual involvement.

Idunn is best known as the keeper of the golden apples,[47] the fruit so vital to the immortality of the gods; the Eddas called Idunn the Renewing One.[48] The place where the apples were kept was in the West, a direction sometimes associated with Maiden goddesses, death, and rebirth.[49] Idunn was the goddess of youth, responsibility, and immortality. Since both She and the Greek Hera guarded apples of immortality, Idunn's name may have come from Ida, the Greek mountain shrine sacred to Hera.

Loki, an evil god, was always causing trouble for the Aesir and Vanir; sometimes he managed to get himself into difficulties. On one of these occasions Loki was captured by a Giant, Thjazi, who refused to let the trickster go unless Loki delivered Idunn and her golden apples to him. Loki was always willing to let another pay for his mistakes, so he kidnapped Idunn and gave Her and the apples to Thjazi. At once the gods began to age. When they discovered Idunn was missing, they turned on Loki who had to rescue the goddess.

Openness (a symbol of youth) and flexibility of the mind and spirit are important qualities of the subconscious and collective unconscious minds. If we are tricked into losing them, into believing that they do not exist or we cannot attain them, we become captives of self-defeating thoughts. These thoughts feed on themselves, luring us into relinquishing our spiritual search for Oneness with the Divine. We begin to dwell on our physical mortality, the false idea that we cannot change or influence our lives; we become depressed and negative in our thinking. In other words, our spiritual thread that twists through the labyrinth begins to slowly disintegrate (age). We need to replenish ourselves with the golden apples, spiritual food for thought.

Parvati of India was the Virgin or Maiden aspect of the goddess Kali. As wife of Shiva, She seduced him when She tired of his asceticism, thus representing the necessary union of god and goddess, man and woman, positive and negative. One sex, one polarity cannot produce or reproduce. Furthermore, it is not the way of the Goddess to practice unusual, harmful, or non-productive austerities. It was said that the passionate embrace of Parvati and Shiva made the whole world tremble. This symbolic picture is similar to the churning or boiling movement of the re-creative cauldron of the Goddess.

Maya, mother of Buddha, was another Virgin aspect of Kali. The same goddess was known to the Greeks as Maia, the virgin mother of Hermes. The Celts knew Her as Maga, the grandmother of Cu Chulainn. Maga or Maj, the May Maiden of Scandinavia, was another of Her forms.[50]

The Chinese Ch'ang-O, or Heng-O, had Her palace of the Great Cold on the Moon, where She lived after fleeing from Her husband I, or Yi, the archer. For a heroic deed of shooting down an excessive number of Suns, the gods had rewarded I with a drink of immortality. The archer was gone for long periods of time from his wife, rambling about the world. Ch'ang-O drank the potion during one of his absences and had to flee when he discovered this. She hid with Hare on the Moon and refused to go home again. She became the keeper of the drink of immortality, which She dispensed only to women.[51]

Parvati and Shiva

The Moon in mythology represents the power of the Feminine, intuition, the psychic, and spiritual knowing. When we learn to listen to these attributes (drink the potion), society and those afraid of or not familiar with these gifts often tend to persecute and ridicule the users. Then we must retreat into the spiritual disciplines we have learned (the Moon) where we have protection. The Maiden goddess Ch'ang-O shows us by Her example that we can receive spiritual protection, but we cannot return to our former unknowing state or go home again.

China also had a Holy Virgin whose first child was a savior; this was Shin-Mu, and Her son was the spirit of the grain. After this divine birth, Shin-Mu birthed thousands of other creatures.[52]

There are other Maiden-type goddesses listed in mythology about whom we know very little. However, the very fact that their names have survived through the centuries is a clue to the importance they once held.

There are few goddesses among the Finnish-Ugrians that can be classified as Maiden deities. One of these is Mielikki, goddess of the forests and woodland animals, bears in particular. She is quite similar to

Artemis as She was called the Goddess of the Hunt. Another was Luon-notar,[53] Daughter of Nature; this goddess was really "daughter of nothing," for, legend says, She existed all alone in the beginning of time before She grew lonesome and created the universe.[54]

Diiwica of the Slavonic Russians may have been derived from the Roman Diana. She too was called the Goddess of the Hunt, ruling over forests, horses, wild animals, and victory.

Iyatiku of the Pueblo Native Americans was Corn Goddess and ruler of the underworld, like the Greek Kore. All the dead came to Her realm. This deity ruled over compassion, agriculture, and children. Onatha of the Iroquois, goddess of wheat and harvest, was also similar to the Greek Kore-Persephone.

The Mayan goddess Ixchup was known as the "Young Moon Goddess" and wife of the Sun. We know this much and little more, but the fact that She is a young phase of the Moon ties Her to the Maiden aspect.

We have a more in-depth picture of Chalchihuitlicue of the Aztecs. As wife of the rain god Tlaloc, She was named "precious green lady," "precious jewel lady," and "precious jade skirt." A goddess of unpredictable temper, Chalchihuitlicue ruled flowers, spring growth, and youthful beauty, among other things.

The virgin mother of the Aztec savior god Quetzalcoatl was Chimalman, one of three holy goddess-sisters.

The faces of the Maiden aspect of the Great Goddess come in as many facets and descriptions as there are cultures around the world. Each facet is slightly different, presenting new thoughts on the Maiden, but the core symbolism remains the same. The Maiden is the Huntress of the mind who, through Her powers of symbolic growth in all its meanings, makes us renew ourselves as a result of our inner journey.

If we are sincere in our inner search through the maze, the Maiden encourages and entices us to follow Her to the Divine Center. She does not send us on by ourselves, but leads the way.

If we are unprepared to face the truth of ourselves, our actions, and our thoughts, if we deny the need for self-improvement and change, the Maiden presents Her terrifying form, complete with writhing snakes and wild hunting hounds. The Huntress then drives us out of the labyrinth, repelling us until we are properly prepared for the inward journey. She protects us from the garbage we have deposited in our subconscious until we can face that jumble of negatives and clean house.

If we go into the labyrinth with an open heart and a truthful desire to find the Divine Center, the Maiden appears as the Keeper of the Keys, the beautiful guardian of the golden apples. With laughter and innocence, She entices us through the maze to our journey's end. No one can hide the truth of the soul from the Maiden, for She is the Prophetess who sees all. She helps us to see ourselves as we really are, but also shows us what we can become spiritually.

PART III
THE MOTHER

VI

THE GODDESS AS MOTHER

I t seems easiest for humankind to recognize, identify with, and call upon the Mother aspect of the Goddess. Physical mothers and the state of motherhood are well known. Because physical mothers tend to be closer to their children than fathers are, the Goddess as Mother seems natural, more accessible.

The Mother aspect of the Goddess is summer, the ripening of all things. She is the re-creation of life, both plant and animal; She is also the creation of universal bodies. She is the high point in all cycles, whether of living or creating, for the Mother blesses and gives with open hands.[1] She is the Great Teacher of the Mysteries. Symbolically, the Mother aspect is the boiling or churning cauldron, the re-creative pot, and the ripeness of womanhood (or adulthood in general). The day, lusti-ness, reproduction, creation in any form and of anything—these are all within Her realm. Traditionally, Her color is red, the color of blood and the life force.

The Mother is associated with adulthood and parenthood. How-ever, as with the other two aspects of the Goddess, Her attributes can be experienced by anyone at any time. Adulthood means the accepting of responsibilities, particularly those brought about by our own actions or commitments. Accepting the results of our own decisions is one of the greatest responsibilities humankind has. Too often we try to slide by this by blaming everything on others. Some psychologists and counselors have not helped the situation; their attitude of "blame everything on the parents" has helped create whole generations of adults who absolve themselves of all responsibility for what they think or do.

By acknowledging the Mother aspect of the Goddess we learn valuable lessons in self-discipline, patience, and responsibility. Mistreating our bodies, whether by excessive food, drugs, alcohol, unsafe sex, too many children, or life-threatening situations, is against Her wishes. Mistreating our minds, and indirectly our bodies, by low self-esteem, staying in abusive situations, allowing others to physically or mentally beat up on us—these also are not within Her desires.

The Goddess as Mother does not require, in fact does not want, Her creations to abuse themselves in any way. She does not like or demand deprivation or immolation; the Mother is ripeness and balance, happiness and enthusiasm for life.

The Mother facet of the Goddess is important to us whenever we need the guidance and energy to finish creating something, whether it is a family or a goal or a spiritual journey. She is the great churning matrix deep within our collective unconscious, the center point of the spiral or circle, the Keeper of the treasure at the end of the labyrinth.

Through the Mother aspect we discover ourselves and our potentials, and learn to take responsibility for our actions. We learn to reach outward to others and inward to the Divine Center, loving and receiving love. It is during this learning phase that we need to understand that every act of love, whether physical, mental, or emotional, is a ritual to the Mother Goddess.

Love extends beyond the physical sexual act, encompassing acts of kindness and spiritual love. The Mother is active working magick, fulfilling the need to make life more comfortable, less demanding, and freer from unnecessary restraints. It is this aspect of love and the Mother that we need to reawaken within our mental realm.

Humans need to realize that those who find it difficult to express love are sadly lacking in the Mother aspect in their lives. By choice, consciously or subconsciously, they have chosen to separate themselves from the Mother, from love, and live in lonely isolation. Most of these people yearn for love, for someone with whom they can share and care. They have lost sight of the Mother's injunction: to be loved, one must know how to love.

The Mother is the embodiment of universal law, the Divine Source of life itself. As the Keeper of spiritual treasure, She sits upon Her throne in the center of the labyrinth, patiently waiting for each individual to find his or her way to Her. Those who try to take shortcuts, who think that a crash course in spirituality will absolve them of self-discipline and the learning of patience, these people will either lose their way in the inner maze or find themselves in a self-created center where the treasure is false. These are the seekers who, in meditation, always hear what they want to hear, and are always told that whatever they are doing is right. Some of these are dangerous individuals who often call themselves masters or gurus, feeding on the energies of those they persuade to follow them. Sooner or later, according to Her own laws, the Mother Goddess will bring them back to reality with a crash.

The Mother is the nurturer of all creation. Her love is unconditional, yet, as with physical mothers, She disciplines when necessary. She has no need, as does the Maiden, to be coy with Her affections; Her sexuality is fully developed, a natural part of life. She is confident in Her independence, going about the business of living while turning a deaf ear to those who think they rule Her. There is no indecision within Her about Her abilities. She knows She is the matrix of all creation, the Keeper of the cycles and seasons. As the Maiden dreams of what She can become, so the Mother knows exactly what She is.

The Mother aspect is the joy of the moment, indeed joy in every moment. Too often we lock ourselves into one phase of the Goddess, thereby missing the growth and experience of the other two. We plunge ourselves into work, whether it be a job, exercise, or "enjoying" ourselves. Everything in life becomes serious. It is no wonder that hypertension and heart problems are death-dealers to humanity. The Goddess dislikes imbalance. She will correct the situation by whatever means necessary if we do not. By studying and meditating upon the Triple Goddess, it is possible to bring our lives back into balance, back to the natural rhythm of Nature, back to sanity and wholeness.

The Mother aspect of the Goddess is synonymous with the adulthood stage of humans. In females, She is the Full Moon or fullness of menstrual life. To males, She is the urge to procreate, to bond with another adult for life-companionship. To both sexes, the Mother aspect is represented by the fully grown sexual drive; the stretching of the mind, body, and spirit in goals; the reveling in the joy of life itself. She is confidence, responsibility, and increasing knowledge of life and the cycles of life.

This stage of the Goddess can be experienced at any human age. If one is still in the physical Maiden stage of life, one can learn to accept responsibility and nurture confidence. If one is in the Crone stage, one can keep working with the Mother through nurturing and creative activities.

The Mother Goddess is the most familiar in all cultures around the world. She comes in many forms and variations, but underneath they are all the same. The Mother is the fullness of life, the Creatress, the Wheel-Turner for the seasons, the divine receptacle of all knowledge. Sometimes She was called Earth Mother, sometimes Sky Mother. She is the divine Teacher at the calm center of the spiritual labyrinth, the One who initiates seekers into the deeper Mysteries. She does not run before us like the Maiden, but walks beside us, hand in hand, whispering revelations and prophecies. Her knowledge is the treasure of the inner maze. The Mother is the Guardian of the Treasure, the Empress of the inner and outer worlds, the High Priestess of all things spiritual. We need Her cooperation or we cannot benefit from the spiritual treasure we find at the Divine Center.

THE MOTHER AND MAGICK

The Mother aspect of the Great Goddess is quite useful in specific types of magick, even candleburning. Summer is the Mother's time of year, the Full Moon Her monthly point of power. Pagan holidays which honor the Mother are Beltane (May 1), Summer Solstice, and Lunasa (August 1). She also rules the Winter Solstice with the Maiden and the Crone. The Christian harvest festival, synonymous with the Pagan Lunasa, has survived in some places and is making a comeback in others.

The Mother type of magick can be used, as can the magick of the Maiden and Crone, with any meditation, candleburning, seed planting, poppet magick, or called upon in any general ritual. The Mother's powers can affect everything from preparing for immanent childbirth to seeking spiritual direction. She is the powerful will to live within humans, the re-creative force that produces a new generation or new thoughts and goals.

Following are examples of rituals that fall within the Mother's domain:

1. Project fruition and completion.
2. When childbirth is near.
3. Strength to see matters through to the end.

4. Blessings and protection. This especially applies to females who are threatened by males.

5. Guidance in life decisions.

6. Marriage, or the contemplation of or desire for marriage.

7. Finding or choosing a mate or companion.

8. Gardening, the growing of any plant.

9. Choosing or accepting an animal. Protection of animal life.

10. Making choices of any kind.

11. Gaining or continuing peace.

12. Developing intuition and psychic gifts.

13. Spiritual direction.

When calling upon the Mother during a candleburning ritual, choose a richly-colored candle of the appropriate shade. Spend adequate time mentally pouring into the candle the problem you wish resolved or the projection you wish to happen. You can even write this out on a small piece of paper to help clarify your desires. Remember, do not use the Mother goddess to cause harm to others; the payback can be heavy. Try to time the ritual for the Full Moon, as Her powers are highest then. Light the candle and place in a safe place to burn out. If you have written your request on paper, burn it in a metal dish.

Another way to honor the Mother and symbolize Her great powers of completion and fulfillment is to plant, tend, and harvest a small garden. It does not have to be more than pots on a terrace; it can be herbs only. Immersing yourself in this activity is a form of worship itself. Feeding the birds and squirrels during the cold winter months is also a gratifying way of showing love and respect for the Mother and Her creatures. So is the patience and love we share with children, the elderly, and all those about us.

It is easiest to relate to and believe in the Mother aspect, since humans intimately know about mothers. The Mother is comfortable and comforting when we need a sympathetic ear and a little nurturing. A mental conversation with Her, or one aloud when you are alone, can bring an instant sense of warmth, love, and peace when nothing and no one else seems to help. The Mother is the most understanding and forgiving of the Triple Goddess aspects.

As the Maiden aspect blends subtly into the Mother and the Crone, so does the Mother blend with the other two. She is separate, yet part of all aspects of the Triple Goddess. The Earth is a visible symbol of Her reproducing body, our home within Her. Her power is boundless, as shown through the cycles of renewal in the seasons. And as Mother of all, She is our will to live, to accomplish, to reproduce, and to establish peace. She lives in all Her creations and creatures, as we do in Her.

VII

WORLD MOTHER
MYTHS

L iterally thousands of goddess names apply to the Mother in various
countries and regions, among them Asia, Africa, Europe, Libya,
Russia, Anatolia, Holland, China, Akka, Chaldea, Scotland, and
Ireland. Because the Great Goddess was most often considered to be
Mother Earth, thus the Great Mother, She has received universal worship. Humans can identify with home and mother, therefore it has been
easy to see the Great Mother as the Earth, our true and only home. At
death, the Crone aspect, She receives all back into Her renewing body to
prepare for rebirth.

The pointed oval is a yonic (female genitals) sign of the Great
Mother worldwide. In Latin it was known as *vesica piscis*, Vessel of the
Fish, because the Hindus said female genitals smelled like fish.[1] In Greek,
fish and womb were the same, and *delphos* meant both.[2] The pre-Hellenic
goddess Themis was often symbolized by a dolphin *(delphinos)*; the Delphic oracle first belonged to Her.

The horseshoe was another widespread yonic symbol. Druidic temples were often built in this shape as are some Hindu shrines. The Greeks
used the horseshoe shape in their alphabet letter Omega; they considered

this the ending of one cycle and the beginning of another, an apt symbol for the mystic phase of reincarnation. Other universal Mother symbols were the cowrie shell and the lily or lotus, all yonic emblems.

The word Ma or Mama is almost a universal word for Great Goddess and Her life-giving fluids or food that sustains all creation. In the beginning of humankind's history, and for centuries after, the blood of the mothers determined kinship.[3] Erich Neumann writes that in Mesopotamia the Great Creatress Goddess was Mami, Mammitu, or Mama. The Hindu goddess Kali was also called Ma, or sometimes Mamaki or Mamata. The first child of the Sumero-Babylonian goddess Tiamat was named Mummu, meaning churning mother. The Hindus called the ancestral matriarchs the Matrikadevis, or Holy Mothers. This term may correspond to the Norse *disir,* the Celtic fairies or feys, and the pre-Hellenic Titans.

Gaea, or Gaia, was an Earth Goddess and Great Mother in Greece. After Themis's reign, the sacred place of Delphi was Hers.[4] She ruled the cauldron, prophecy, and motherhood. Gaea, the Deep-Breasted One, was the oldest of the divinities. Although Zeus and other male gods took over Her shrines, the gods swore all their oaths in Her name, as subjects of Her law. In Thrace, at Her mountain shrines, Gaea was called Pangaea and Panorma.

In the beginning was Chaos, the vast, dark void, and Gaea, the broad-bosomed Earth. Gaea birthed then mated with Uranus, the sky. Some of their children were the Titans Cronus, Oceanus, Rhea, Phoebe, and Themis, the ancestors of humankind, the arts, and magick. As soon as the Cyclops, the storm gods, were born, Uranus shut them up inside Gaea. The Goddess, angry at this insult and control, made a sickle and persuaded Her youngest son Cronus to castrate his father. After doing this, Cronus freed the other Titans and became their leader. They all interbred, finishing creation and producing a host of other deities.

Chaos is very likely another synonym for Gaea as Great Mother. Thus She mated with Herself and produced a three-way division of the universe, a symbol of the Triple Goddess: sky as Maiden, Earth as Mother, dark void as Crone. The Maiden, or sky, did not like the unpredictable emotions loosed in the form of the Cyclopic storm gods. So She, as Uranus, locked the storm gods, the unpleasant lessons of life and their consequences, inside the physical; this may well be a metaphor for the subconscious mind buried within the conscious. Gaea as Mother took Her sickle (the Moon and its influences on humans) and instructed Cronus (the fearful yet enterprising aspect of humanity) to free them. This freedom (castration) brought forth Aphrodite, or the matrix that created physical love between the sexes, and also set humans on the path of learning through life experiences. A natural outcome of the division of humans into two sexes would be the finishing of creation by reproducing and becoming civilized.

The Cretan goddess Rhea was the Aegean Great Goddess long before the Greek patriarchal clans moved into the Mediterranean area. As the Cretan archetypal Triple Goddess, She reigned supreme without a consort. In Hellenic myth She was given a consort, Cronus or Time, which was one of Her own titles (Mother Time, or Rhea Kronia). Rhea may be the same goddess as Rha, the Red One of Russia, and the Celtic Rhiannon.

Together, Cronus and Rhea produced Hestia, Demeter, Hera, Hades, Poseidon, and Zeus. There was a prophecy that his children would supplant him, so at each birth Cronus swallowed the child. Rhea saved Zeus, the last child, by substituting a rock for him; this Cronus swallowed at once. The infant Zeus was hidden in a cave on Crete where he was raised by nymphs. When Zeus was strong enough, he persuaded a Titan daughter of Oceanus to mix a potion which caused Cronus to vomit up the rest of the children. Then Zeus chained Cronus in the depths of the heavens. The Titans, except for a few, warred against the new deities; the ten-year battle ended with the Titans being chained in Tartarus, the depths of the Earth. After gaining control of all the deities, Zeus raped his mother Rhea.

Cronus has a connection with both the Crone and time. Rhea also means time, as well as Mother Earth. The Crone, or time, swallows each life, whatever it is, at the end of its cycle. The matrix of that life rests within Her until the right set of circumstances causes Her to vomit it forth in a new cycle. Zeus, as the divine life spark, is spared the womb-tomb destruction; when the proper key (potion) is found, the divine life spark joins with the resting matrix to create for the next cycle.

The chaining of Cronus symbolizes that nothing can be totally destroyed, yet some actions and emotions must be controlled. The warring Titans are the primitive, uncontrolled emotions, ever-present in the mind, which must not be allowed to gain the upper hand. Although they are chained in Tartarus, the deep areas of the subconscious, they are still alive. It is up to each individual to keep them under control. In people such as murderers, rapists, thieves, abusers, etc., these primitive emotions are allowed unrestricted freedom. Zeus's rape of his mother is, of course, a later patriarchal addition.

The Greek goddess Demeter had an ancient cult center in Mycenae. The tombs there had triangular doors, short passages, and round domes, all symbolic of the womb of the Goddess. The triangular doors also represented Demeter's trinity with Kore-Persephone and Hecate. She was worshipped throughout Greece well into the nineteenth century.[5] Her temple at Eleusis was one of the greatest in Greece and was the site of an intense mystery-religion. During these rites, the Divine Child was symbolically killed and resurrected. All those taking part in these mysteries were called Demetreioi, blessed ones of Demeter.[6]

In Greece, the word *meter* means mother, and *de* is delta or triangle, the symbol for the female genitals.[7] In Mycenae and Crete, Demeter was also known as horse-headed, Her dual names being Leukippe (white mare of life) and Melanippe (black mare of death).

In Phrygia, Samothrace, and other areas, Demeter was called Cabiria, or the Goddess of the Cabirian Mysteries. These rituals were second only to those of Eleusis in mystical importance.

The Roman goddess Ceres was identified with the Greek Demeter, an Earth Mother and Grain Goddess. The word "cereal" comes from Her name. The story of Ceres and Her daughter Proserpina is the same as that of Demeter and Kore-Persephone. But She was also considered to be the Lawgiver; Her priestesses were said to be the founders of the Roman legal system.[8] Her festival was the Cerealia, one form of which was said to have been practiced in Britain until the late nineteenth century.

Hera (Holy One) was queen of the Greek gods on Olympus; the title Hiera was used by ancient queens who ruled in Her name. Hera was a surviving goddess of an earlier Aegean civilization and matriarchy.[9] She married Her brother Zeus against Her will; there was an unending battle between them over his constant chasing of other women, mortal and immortal. At Her marriage, Hera was given a special magick garden in the West where She kept Her apples of immortality. This magickal garden was called the Hesperides, probably a symbol of Her regenerating womb; Her apples were guarded by Her sacred serpent. It was also said that Hera controlled the ambrosia of the gods.[10] The peacock, labrys (double-axe), and sickle were among Her emblems.

The Roman Juno was the equivalent of Hera, often being called Juno Augusta. Her name, however, may have been derived from the Sabine-Etruscan goddess Uni, the Three-in-One. As the Great Mother, Juno was honored as the national Goddess.[11] The Romans said that every female embodied a piece of this goddess, the female soul, which they called a *juno*. Peacock feathers with their iridescent colors and "eyes" were symbolic of Her watchfulness and justice which judged the souls of humans.

The month of June was sacred to Juno as goddess of marriage and family, a tradition still subconsciously respected. As harvest deity, She was later connected with the European festival of Lunasa; by one name or another, Juno, Ops, Ceres, and Demeter were honored at harvest throughout the Middle Ages. The month of August was also sacred to Juno, with the term "august" being applied to oracles.

The Etruscan goddess Uni meant the Triple Goddess, the three in one, who birthed the universe. Uni may have been derived from the word yoni, or female genitals. In Rome She was known as Juventas,[12] the Maiden aspect of the triad of Juno and Minerva. Under patriarchal influence She was replaced by Jove, or Jupiter.

Aphrodite, Greek goddess of love, among other things, was said to be older than time.[13] In Her Middle Eastern version as Asherah or Astarte, She had the oldest continuously operated temple in the world. Since She, under the name of Venus, gave birth to Aeneas, the Romans considered Her their ancestral mother. The city of Venice is named after Her. The island of Cyprus, noted for its copper mines, was one of Her major worship centers; Aphrodite's sacred metal is copper. In Her shrine at Mount Eryx, Her high priestess was called Melissa, or Bee; Her emblem there was a golden honeycomb.

This goddess ruled birth, life, love, death, time, and fate. Through certain sacred sexual rites Her priestesses initiated humans into Her mysteries. Under the Roman name of Venus, this goddess primarily represented sex in all its applications. Since She was born of the ocean foam that arose after Cronus cast down his father's severed genitals, Aphrodite was also called the goddess of the sea. Frogs were associated with Venus, as they were with Hecate and the Egyptian goddess Hekat.[14]

Although Ilithyia was considered a separate goddess who ruled over childbirth, the same name was applied to Aphrodite, Diana, Artemis, Isis, Buto, Hathor, Nephthys, and others. Ilithyia was said to be the Liberator who freed the child from the womb.

Under the name of Androphonos (Man-slayer), Aphrodite was the Destroyer, the Black One, Goddess of Tombs. The patriarchal conquerors tried to turn Her into only a goddess of love, thus negating Her complex role in the Goddess triad.

Ariadne, of the tale of Theseus and the bull ring at Crete, was really another form of the Cretan Moon goddess Britomartis. Her name means "High Fruitful Mother"; Graves wrote that She was the consort of Dionysus.[15] Images of Her with snakes (symbolizing rebirth) in Her hands represent Her oracular priestesses; the bare breasts may symbolize the sexual nature of Her rituals.

The Moon goddess Selene, or Mene, was specifically associated with the second phase of the Moon, or its full aspect. She was the sister of Helios, the Sun god. The woodland god Pan fell in love with Her and, in the form of a white ram, enticed Her into the forests of Arcadia. Zeus granted Selene's mortal lover, Endymion, immortality on the condition he lay in eternal sleep.

Themis, Earth Mother and mother of the Fates, was the deity of law and order; She protected the innocent and punished the guilty. This goddess is an apt symbol of the collective unconscious.

The Roman Tellus Mater was a very ancient Earth Goddess and fertility deity; Her consort was Telluno. Marriage, family, and children were under Her rule. A bride sacrificed to Her upon entering the new husband's house. Tellus Mater was also an agricultural deity, protecting the fruitfulness of the soil and planted crops.

One of the Mother goddesses of Egypt was Hathor, mother of all deities and goddess of the Moon. Originally She was called Het-Hert, or

Tellus Mater

Hat-Hor, meaning the House or Womb of Horus. As with many goddesses, Hathor was self-created.[16] She was also called queen of the West, or the dead. Her celebration was New Year's Day. Hathor protected women in general and motherhood in particular. Egyptians called Hathor the heavenly cow who made the Milky Way from Her life-giving fluids. This goddess was identified with the legendary Nile Goose who laid the Golden Egg of the Sun.[17]

Hathor also had a darker side, that of the avenging Mother. In the beginning when humankind was new upon the Earth, the Sun god Ra decided to punish humans because they became wicked and disrespectful. He called Hathor to carry out his decree. Turned loose upon the Earth, the goddess slew until blood ran in rivers. When Ra decided the punishment was sufficient, he called for Hathor to stop. Aroused in Her anger, She refused. At last, Ra set out 7,000 jars of beer spiked with mandrake to resemble blood. Hathor drank them all, became very drunk, and forgot Her battle fever.

The subconscious mind has both the ability to create and to destroy. In creating, it can bring forth amazing ideas to benefit society or change a personality into a more positive mode. In destroying, it can invent ways to make life miserable or encourage destructive habits that wreck lives. However, no one has the luxury of breaking spiritual laws and not paying the price. Only by returning through the labyrinth to the calm center can one refocus one's life and regain the peace of the Great Mother. Only by recognizing the price we must pay for our mistakes (the blood-beer sacrifice) and becoming "drunk" with spirit can we move away from negative emotions and actions.

Isis is probably the best known of Egyptian goddesses. She was called the Great Mother and was also associated with the Moon. The Greeks identified Her with Demeter, Hera, and Selene. To the Egyptians, Isis was part of a triad with Osiris and Horus, but this was very likely a later designation that replaced two female deities. Her name, "throne-woman," relates Her to the Great Serpent Ua Zit. She was called the Creatress and the Giver of Life, titles which applied to many Egyptian goddesses. Isis was considered the weaver and knotter of the life threads, or fate, of each individual. The Knot of Fate (the Tat, or Tait) was used for creating magick with knots; holy mysteries were called *shetat*, "she-knots."[18] She was connected with cats, marriage, motherhood, initiations, and civilizations. Sometimes She was shown with winged arms.

When Osiris, the brother/consort of Isis, was killed and dismembered by the evil Set, Isis used Her magick to find and repair the body, then animate it long enough to get pregnant. The resulting child was Horus, the god whose eyes were the Sun and the Moon, the avenger for his mother. Thoth finally had to see that a balance was kept between Horus and Set because of their repeated violent confrontations.

There must be a balance of male (Osiris) and female (Isis), positive and negative, active and receptive, within each mind for creative purposes. There are certain types of controlling people who do not want this knowledge to be revealed, who wage wars on physical and mental levels to keep this creative energy from being used. But the negative and positive always have an attraction for each other; their offspring are the vindication of this attraction. True knowledge and wisdom (Thoth) sees that a balance is kept, the cycles of being observed. The Mother's laws decree that balance of the body, mind, and spirit are essential to inner and outer peace. The wisdom of seeing the truth keeps this balance, even if we are plagued by outside interference.

Mut[19] was the Great Mother sky goddess who usually wore a vulture headdress. She was self-produced. Some myths claim that Isis and Osiris were born from Mut's womb; Her hieroglyphic sign was three cauldrons, representing the Triple Womb.[20] Three cauldrons, the cow, cat, and lioness were among Her emblems.

Nut,[21] or Nu, was similar to Rhea; She was called the Mother of all gods. She was the night sky and, as the Cosmic Cow, Her milk made the Milky Way.[22] Usually She was shown as a woman arched on Her fingers and toes over the phallic Earth god, Her consort. When painted inside the lids of coffins, Nut's arms were stretched to embrace the dead.

In one of the Egyptian myths, Nut and Her brother/consort Seb spent so much time copulating that Ra ordered they be separated. By this time Nut was heavily pregnant with several children, but could not give birth until Thoth won enough extra days and light for Her to do so.

In a spiritual interpretation, the re-creative powers within all creatures must move in cycles, whether this be physical, mental, or spiritual activities. There must be a time when the seed is planted (copulation); however, too many seeds should not be planted at one time. Then comes a time of rest (pregnancy). When knowledge and wisdom (Thoth) are gained, there comes a time of birth, or completion of projects. Too many times we plant our minds with far too many mental or spiritual ideas for our own good, without taking a time of rest to assimilate them. Then we feel over-full, too pregnant. We must rest, giving our subconscious and collective unconscious minds time to grow the seeds. We need to learn and gain the knowledge necessary to bring them to fruition.

The hippo goddess Ta-Urt, or Taueret, was primarily a Mother goddess of childbirth and pregnancy. Sometimes She was an avenging deity; in this aspect She had a hippo body with the head of a lioness.

The Middle East was filled with goddesses representing the Mother aspect of the Great Goddess. Asherah was the Semitic name of the Great Goddess. Because of Her great wisdom, She was called Mistress of the gods, Holy Mother, and Mother of the gods. Her sacred city was Marash.[23] Her sacred groves, where Her priestesses initiated people through sacred sexual rites, were attacked and condemned by the Hebrews.

Astarte, the Lady of Byblos, is one of the oldest forms of the Great Goddess in the Middle East. She is similar to Hathor, Demeter, and Aphrodite. Her sacred shrine at Byblos dates back to the Neolithic Age. Byblos was noted for its extensive libraries before they were destroyed; the word "bible" comes from the name of this center. The kings of Sidon ruled only with Her permission and each was called the Priest of Astarte. As queen of heaven, She wore crescent horns and was said to tirelessly create and destroy. Astarte was called the Mother of all souls, giving starry (astral) bodies to the reborn. The Syrians and Egyptians held Her sacred drama of birthing the Sun god on December 25.[24] Other cultures in the Middle East knew Astarte as Asherat of the Sea or Ashtart,[25] queen of heaven.

Inanna, as queen of heaven and Earth and goddess of battle, incorporated both the Mother and Crone aspects in Her powers of love and war. Every Sumerian king could come to the throne only through marriage to Her. She was considered the source of the Earth's blood, the water of wells, rivers, and springs. In one legend, Inanna was said to descend into the underworld to rescue Her lover/consort Dumuzi; this shows Her, along with Her connection with water, to also be a fertility goddess. In another version of the legend She went to the underworld to search for wisdom and knowledge. Returning, She found Her consort Dumuzi usurping Her throne, so She condemned him to take Her place in the land of the dead. The Hittites knew Her as Inaras; they said She annually renewed Her virginity as the bride of the specially chosen sacred king at the festival of Purulli. This festival later became the Jewish Purim.

Ishtar, lady of heaven, goddess of the Moon, the Great Mother, was a goddess of both positive and negative qualities. The Babylonians knew this goddess as the Light of the World, Opener of the Womb, Lawgiver, Lady of Victory, etc.[26] She was the sister of Ereshkigal, the underworld goddess. An annual festival celebrated Her descent into the underworld to bring forth Her son/lover Tammuz; this festival lasted three days with

Ishtar

sacrifices and atonement for sins, ending in the Day of Joy which began a new year.[27] Ishtar had a lion throne and double serpent scepter; sometimes She was pictured accompanied by dragons. Like the Norse Freyja, Ishtar has a rainbow necklace and was associated with sexual love.

According to the legend of the hero Gilgamesh, Ishtar fell in love with Tammuz, god of the harvest. Her love was fatal to Tammuz, but the goddess mourned his death so much that She decided to go into the underworld to bring him back. Down Ishtar went into the darkness. In order to pass through each of the seven gates, She had to leave behind one piece of adornment. When She finally reached the palace of Her sister Ereshkigal, queen of the dark land, Ishtar stood naked before Her. Ereshkigal imprisoned Her sister and tortured Her. It took the powerful magick words of Asushu-Namir, messenger from the great Ea, to free Her. Ea also decreed that Tammuz could spend part of the year with Ishtar, but must return to the land of the dead the rest of the time. Ishtar was sprinkled with the water of life, and during Her ascent to the surface, She retrieved each piece of jewelry and clothing at the seven gates.

This myth has several layers of meaning. First, it is a surface story of the Great Mother and the yearly cycle of vegetation, much as with Demeter and Kore-Persephone. Second, it portrays a journey into the subconscious and collective unconscious minds. In the course of a life cycle we are dealt blows which cause us great sadness: the loss of a loved one, a divorce, arguments with family, illness, the defeat of a cherished plan, a series of chaotic happenings that leave little hope. We begin to withdraw from life. Whether we realize it or not, we are making the descent through the inner labyrinth into the underworld to either win a new outlook on life or give up all together.

As we descend, either emotionally or deliberately through meditation, we must pass through the seven gates (chakras), releasing some cherished thing (emotionally or metaphorically) at each. When we finally stand before the Divine Center, we are naked; everything about us is totally revealed. At this point it takes magick words, the power of our own will, to set us free; no one else can do this for us. The Great Mother will lend us support, encouragement, and spiritual aid, but even She will not interfere with our necessary growth process.

As we come back up through each of the gates, we discover that the treasured things we left behind are still there, as good as new or transformed for the better. A part of us will still mourn the loss we suffered—that is part of the cycle of life. But we now have that loss under control.

Tanit, or Tanith, was similar to Ishtar. She was a Moon goddess and Great Goddess. This was Ishtar's name in the city of Carthage.

Jahi the Whore was a goddess of the Moon, menstruation, and sex. The Persians said Jahi mated with the serpent Ahriman and brought menstruation into the world. Therefore, since all women descended from Jahi, all women were whores to the Persians.

Lilith was the Feminine Principle of the universe. The patriarchal writers of the Bible cut Her from their history, but She was called Adam's first wife. Tradition says that Lilith left Adam because he demanded full control of sexual positions. Originally, this goddess ruled over pregnancy and sexual love, with the owl as Her symbol. Patriarchy changed Her into a demoness who preyed on pregnant women and newborns. It is possible that the name Lilith came from the Sumero-Babylonian goddess Belit-ili or Belili. A tablet from Ur, about 2,000 BCE, mentions the name Lillake.[28]

There were two goddesses whose names are quite similar and may, in fact, be the same. Nammu, or Ama, was called the Creatress Mother of the gods and was connected with the sea. Nanna was portrayed with a fish or serpent tail, associated with the Moon, and called the Great Mother.

The Babylonian goddess Nanshe was the interpreter of dreams, the giver of the ability to prophesy. As part of their initiation, Her priests had

Lilith

to descend into a pit for a time of contemplation, symbolic of returning to Her re-creative womb and being reborn.

The goddess Ninhursag was the Great Mother, Earth Mother, and the Creative Principle of the universe; She made the first humans out of clay. Serpents were sacred to Her. She dealt with regeneration, reincarnation, and the life principle in general.

The Philistine goddess Atargatis was identified in many ways with Aphrodite. She was portrayed with a fish-tail, like a mermaid; at Her sacred temple in Harran, special fish were used in divinatory practices. She was called Derceto the Whale in Babylon. The Christian-Hebrew tale of Jonah was taken from the Babylonian myth of Atargatis birthing Oannes; the Philistines called Oannes by the name of Dagon.

Official worship of Cybele was brought to Rome from Phrygia in about 204 BCE following an order of the Cumaean Sybil, a Roman priestess and prophetess of the cave-dwelling goddess. Cybele was considered the Great Mother of the gods. It is said that until the fourth century CE Her temple in Rome stood where St. Peter's Basilica stands today. Along with Hecate and Demeter of Eleusis, Cybele was a leading deity of the Mystery-Religions.[29] Her sacred caves were known as marriage bowers, referring to Her connection with Her consort Attis. Cybele was an Earth and Great Mother Goddess; some of her symbols were bees, sickles, lions, cymbals, pomegranates, and the scourge.

The Sanskrit root word for Goddess was Devi. This shows up in many goddess names of Indo-European ancestry. This is particularly true of many goddess names in India, where Devi was called the Dearly Beloved, or the Shakti. As Devayani, She was the Divine Yoni, or the Way to the Gods.

Aditi was known as Mother of the gods in Indian mythology, but Sarasvati was called Mother of the Vedas. Aditi was the Great Mother, the Sun goddess who birthed the twelve zodiacal Adityas.

Sarasvati was the wife of Brahma and goddess of learning and the creative sciences, speech, poetry, and music. She was said to have invented all the arts of civilization. She may have originally been a river goddess since Her waters were said to bless and confer divinity on baptized kings; however, it is more likely that the waters referred to were menstrual blood. Under the name of Savitri, She brought forth death and all diseases.

Uma

Tara

The Corn Goddess Uma[30] was sometimes known as the Mother aspect of the triad including Parvati and Kali. This position is not clear, since Durga is also known as the Mother.

The Vedas tell of a mare-goddess, Saranyu, who was mother of the Asvins or centaurs, the physician gods. The mating which produced the Asvins occurred in much the same way as the mating between Demeter and Poseidon. Saranyu also gave birth to Yama, Lord of Death, and Yami, Lady of Life.

The Hindu goddess Lakshmi, deity of abundance and prosperity, was shown seated on or holding a lotus, an emblem of spiritual purity and fertility. She was considered the divine principle that gave all creation vitality, consciousness, and will. In order for Indra to proclaim himself as king of the gods, Lakshmi gave him a drink of *soma* (wise blood) from Her own body.

Durga, the Queen-Mother, or another Mother aspect of the Indian Goddess trinity, was usually depicted as an Amazon-type warrioress who defeated demons for the gods. As the Inaccessible, Durga represented the mother's fighting instincts to preserve her offspring. She was invoked on the sixth day after childbirth. Durga-Devi, as a symbol of cosmic harmony, is also said to restore world order and bring peace to individuals in any time of crisis.

The goddess Tara, the Universal Mother, was familiar in both India and Tibet; She was also known in two forms, White Tara and Green Tara. In India, Tara was a pre-Vedic goddess, the first, oldest, and greatest. The White Tara symbolizes purity, fulfillment of wishes, and good luck. The Green Tara of seven all-seeing eyes[31] is said to grant spiritual and material requests. Some form of this goddess was recognized from India to Ireland;[32] Dumezil lists several deity names that are linked with Tara: the Latin Terra Mater, Hebrew Terah, Gaul Taranis, and Etruscan Turan.

China also had several Mother goddesses. Nu Kua, or Nuwa, was the Creatress goddess of humans; in early sources She was pictured with the lower body of a serpent.[33] Hsi Wang Mu was called queen of the West and the highest goddess; She kept the peaches of immortality in an orchard in the West, much the same as Idunn and Hera did their apples. Pi-Hsia Yuan-Chin was the goddess of good fortune, but more importantly, goddess of childbirth. Hu-Tu, or Hou-T'u, was an Earth and fertility deity.

The most popular and best known for centuries was Kuan Yin, or Kwan Yin, the Great Mother, goddess of mercy, motherhood, childbirth,

Kuan Yin

and the giver of children. She is said to rescue supplicants from danger and suffering. In some images She is pictured with androgynous features, symbolizing the balance of opposites, yin and yang, which creates inner peace. Kuan Yin (Yoni of yonis) was sometimes pictured as a fish-goddess.[34]

To the Japanese, Izanami was the Female Principle of creation, an Earth goddess and Great Goddess. With Her consort Izanagi, She created the islands of Japan and many deities. The last child, god of Fire, killed Her and She descended to Hell. Izanagi went after Her, much as Ishtar did Tammuz, but Izanagi ran away in fright, leaving Izanami there.

Amaterasu was one of the few Sun goddesses,[35] a Great Goddess who ruled over all Japanese deities. The imperial family traced their lineage from Her. She was known as Mother Creation-Spirit.

Kishi-mojun was the Universal Mother, deity of fertility. Her origin was China where She was a demoness who devoured children. Stories say that after Her conversion by Buddha She protected and healed children. The Shingon sect who brought Her to Japan kept Her original name, Kariteimo.

Mader-Akka, or Mother Akka, was the Creatress of humans to the Lapps and Finns, as was Ilmater, the Sky Mother and Creatress. The goddess Rauni was the lightning goddess and Earth/Forest Mother (particularly of rowan trees).

The story of Ilmater, daughter of Air, is told in the Kalevala. The East wind made Her pregnant with the hero Vainamoinen. She floated upon the vast primeval waters for seven centuries, unable to give birth because there was no land. At last the highest god Ukko sent a teal to build a nest; the broken eggs from this nest were made by the creative powers of the goddess into the Earth, sky, Sun, Moon, and clouds. However, She continued to carry the child for thirty summers before his birth.

Air and the East are traditionally the direction of the mind and its creative mental and magickal powers. The mind (a separate entity from the brain) floats constantly in a fertile sea of creative ability, but we must give ideas a chance to grow or ripen (represented by the seven centuries and thirty summers). Inspiration from spirit (the teal) creates a foundation (nest) for these ideas. We must go through the labor pains of birthing the idea alone. We are given opportunities, but never anything whole without work of some kind.

To the Slavonic Russian culture, Mati Syra Zemlya was the Great Mother and an Earth goddess. Her name translates as "Moist Mother Earth." Slavonic peasants continued to worship Her even after orthodox Christianity gained control. They petitioned Her in matters of weather, protection, and the dead.

Kupala was the Slavonic goddess known as the Water Mother. Like both Aphrodite and Hera, Kupala annually renewed Her virginity by bathing in a sacred spring. Her worshippers believed they could purify their souls with the dew collected on the eve of Her great festival, from all indications Summer Solstice.

The only Old Russian goddess to hold a prominent place was Mokosh, who spun the threads of a person's life. She was portrayed with a large head and long arms. Her image was continued in the figure of St. Paraskeva, a mother-protectress who held power over health, harvests, and stock fertility.

The first Great Mother of the Norse mythology was Audhumla, the cosmic cow who licked the first Giant out of the all-pervading ice that covered Her universal abode.

After the creation of the gods, the world, and people, the god Heimdall mated with three females and thus were produced the three races of humans. The Norse woman-goddess Amma gave birth to the race of *karls*, or freemen. Erda, or Edda (Mother Earth), gave birth to the *thralls*, or slaves; Her name means "Great-Grandmother." Modir, the Mother, birthed the

Mokosh

ruling class of *jarls* (earls), or landowners; since Her name in German means a mixture of earth and water, Modir may be the same as the Slavonic Mati Syra Zemlya.

Freyja of the Vanir, also known as the Vanadis, was considered the leader of the *disir*, the Divine Matriarchs.[36] These feminine deities had ruled the clans before the patriarchal pantheon of the Aesir took over. The Norse said that the *disir* and Vanir knew the only true magick, that the Aesir learned all the magick they knew from Freyja.[37] Friday was Freyja's day, later condemned as unlucky by Christian monks; since both Friday and the number 13 were connected with the Great Goddess, they were propagandized as extremely unlucky when they fell together. The Pagans, however, thought that without this goddess nothing was lucky, as shown by the myths.[38] Her cats, Bygul and Trjegul, pulled Her chariot.

Freyja had many other titles and functions. In Her position as leader of the Valkyries, She claimed half of the slain as Her own. As Mardoll (Moon Shining on the Sea), She was the Creatress of the primeval waters. As Syr, She was a seeress and the death-sow. As the Sage or sayer, Freyja inspired all sacred poetry. Wise women, seeresses, rune-mistresses and healers were closely connected with this goddess, as She was the deity of magick, Witchcraft, and love affairs (these affairs did not necessarily lead to marriage).

Her secret magick, or Witchcraft, was known as *seidr*.[39] This magick was shamanistic in nature, as represented by Her falcon cape, which enabled Her to shape-shift into a bird, travel to the underworld, and return with prophecies. Present-day shamans still consider this ability necessary in order to heal or predict the future. Seidr was a form of magick, trance, and divination that originated with Freyja and was basically a feminine mystical craft. It was fairly independent of runic magick, being more involved with shape-shifting, astral body travel through the nine worlds, sex magick, and other techniques. Her female human followers, called *volvas*, sometimes *seidkona*, were consulted on all manner of problems, whether the volvas were alive or dead.[40]

Women were not the exclusive workers of Freyja's seidr. There are hints in the poems and prose that at one time seidr was also practiced by men. If a male practiced this magick, he had to dress as a woman. This does not mean he was homosexual; cross-dressing is a very ancient tradition that has its roots in the belief that a man has to spiritually become a woman in order to serve the Goddess. However, this was not a popular occupation with men.

Freyja possessed a magickal falcon cloak or skin which enabled Her to fly, and the extremely valuable necklace Brisingamen. Her falcon cloak is a metaphor for astral traveling; even among present-day shamans some physical or mental object is the focal point for the beginning of astral travel. Necklaces have been associated with the Mother Goddess as far back as 3,000 BCE. The circle of the necklace symbolizes the vaginal opening or creative powers.

Snorri Sturluson mentions that Freyja was once married to the mysterious god Od who disappeared. For him, She wept tears of gold; tradition says that the tears that fell into the sea became amber.

The Eddaic poem Grimnismal says that She was connected with war and the world of the dead, dividing those killed in battle with Odin. Half the slain warriors went to Valhalla and half went to Sessrumnir, Her hall on Folkvang (Field of Folk).

Frigg, a Mother Goddess and wife of Odin, is a rather vague, mysterious deity in the myths, except for Her involvement in trying to protect Her son Balder. In fact, some interpreters say She may be an aspect of Freyja; a slang term of Her name means to make physical love.[41] She was sometimes called Frigga or Fricca.[42] In the Lokasenna this goddess was said to know the fate of every being but says nothing and generally interferes in no life, except when She tried to save Her son Balder from his destiny and when She influenced Geirrod.

Frigg is the custodian of ancient wisdom, a form of the Universal Mother, all-powerful and wise, giving comfort especially to women in labor.[43] Since Frigg's magickal symbol was the distaff, it is possible that originally She spun the life-thread for the Norns, who then wove the spiritual fabric of a person's life. Since almost all myths and deities deal with more than one level of understanding, the power of Frigg can be said to also deal with the birth of spiritual children, or ideas and creative projects.

Frigg's powers primarily influenced the future or the destiny of an individual. The Norse peoples believed that no one could completely change the destiny handed down by the Norns at birth; however, they did believe that destiny could often be influenced by courage, certain positive actions, and help from the gods. In Grimnismal is the story of two brothers, Geirrod and Agnar. Odin supports Geirrod as the candidate to inherit a kingdom, while Frigg supports Agnar. In this tale Frigg directly takes a hand in influencing Geirrod to show his true character, which he does by torturing the disguised Odin when the god visits his hall. Thus Agnar gains the kingdom, while Geirrod is killed. Frigg does not blatantly influence this situation like her husband Odin would have; instead she works behind the scenes to bring out the true character of Geirrod, who reveals himself to be an unworthy candidate for leadership of the kingdom.

Invoking the goddess Frigg is invoking the use of primal creative matter in the spiritual realms. By gently applying magickal pressure at various points in your life, you can subtly alter parts of your destiny. This magickal application can be done on an external level, such as working to relieve material problems, or on an internal level, such as correcting negative personality traits. But the greatest lesson learned from Frigg is knowing what can be changed and what cannot be changed, and finding the courage and strength to persevere anyway.

Nanna, the Earth Mother and wife of Balder, is also a vague deity. Nerthus, sometimes called Erce (Earth), was another Mother goddess.

Sif, wife of Thorr, with Her long golden hair is probably symbolic of the Earth Mother, fertility, and the harvest. There was great turmoil when Loki cut off Sif's hair, a symbol of disaster destroying the life-giving harvest and the regenerating qualities of the Earth.

Badb of Ireland was considered the Mother aspect of a triad with Anu and Macha. Her boiling cauldron is a symbol of the universal womb of regeneration and the matrix of life. Badb was noted for Her accurate prophecies. If we open ourselves to the spiritual, we are presented with hunches, intuitions, dreams, etc. which can prepare us for the future.

The Irish goddess Danu was called the Mother, as shown by the name of some Irish peoples in mythology, the Tuatha de Danaan.[44] The Russians knew this goddess by the name Dennitsa, or Greatest of Goddesses. Danu was masculinized under the name Don in the later Irish legends.[45] This goddess's name also surfaces in the Greek Danae, mother of Perseus.

The Celtic name for Ireland was, and still is in some places, Eire or Erinn, a name related to that of the goddess Eriu. As mentioned in the legends, Eriu was a daughter of the Dagda and part of a trinity with Banba and Fotia.[46] Eriu may well be a form of Hiera, or Hera.[47] The title Erua was also applied to the Babylonian goddesses Ishtar and Inanna.

The Celtic goddess Epona, "The Great Mare," was probably modeled after the Cretan Leukippe, a form of Demeter. Her area of worship stretched from Spain to Eastern Europe, Italy to Britain. The hillside horses may have been carved in Her honor.[48]

Arthurian romances also portray a Mother deity in subdued form. This was Margawse; She mated with Her brother Arthur and produced his nemesis Mordred. If one looks at the story of Arthur from a mythological viewpoint, it becomes the tale of a sacrificial king displaced by a challenger.

Another Mother aspect of the Arthur story was Guinevere, the Triple Goddess Gwenhwyfar of the Welsh Triads.[49] Because of Her many abductions, it would appear that no man could be king of Britain without Guinevere as his wife.

In Africa, there were a great many goddesses who fit the Mother aspect. Unfortunately, not many of the myths describing these goddesses have survived in their complete state. Asase Yaa was the Creatress, the Earth Goddess who also received the dead. Nana Buluku, the mother of Mawu, was called Creatress of the world. Nzambi, a Great Goddess, was known as the Creatress and punisher of all. Oddudua was a primary Mother Goddess. The best known is probably Mawu, the supreme Creatress who was connected with the Moon. Many times Mawu and Lisa were said to be joint female deities. The deity Lisa was sometimes recognized as female, sometimes male. This indecisiveness may point to Lisa being originally female, with later patriarchal changes of sex.

The Pacific cultures abounded with Mother and Crone images. Those of the Mother aspect were Aponibolinayen of the Philippines, a Moon and sky goddess; the Creatress Atanea of Micronesia; the Creatress Koevasi of Melanesia; La'i-La'i, also a Creatress, of Hawaii; and Papa, Earth Mother of Polynesia. Wahini-Hai, the Polynesian Creatress of the world and Mother Goddess was also called the Moon and the first woman;[50] Joseph Campbell says that Her name was used in the word *wahine*, meaning woman. She had protruding eyes and a tongue that hung to Her feet; myths say that She stole and ate small children.[51]

The Aborigines of Australia had several goddesses of the Mother type: the Djanggawul Sisters, Creatresses; the Junkgowa Sisters, also Creatresses; Kunapipi, a Great Mother goddess; and Imberombera, a Great Mother deity. Julunggul, better known as the Great Rainbow Snake, was an androgynous creator.

Among the Native Americans, legends of Mother goddesses have not been well preserved. However, a few of their names are known to us: Ataentsic of the Iroquois and Huron, who was called Great Mother; Nokomis of the Algonquin, an Earth goddess; Yolkai Estasan of the Navaho, who was also considered an Earth goddess; Sedna of the Inuit (Eskimo) cultures, who was goddess of the sea, hunting, and sorcery, a type of Mother-Crone; and Spider Woman of the southwestern peoples. To the Apache, Changing Woman (also called White-Painted Woman or White Shell Woman) was a goddess who founded the Apache culture and ruled over the puberty rites for girls. The Navajo's Changing Woman was considered the Earth and its changing seasons; She is said to live in a magnificent house in the West.

Coatlicue

Mexico had a goddess similar to Demeter. She was Chicomecoatl, Heart of the Earth, and considered the ancestress of all people. Her messengers were seven serpents. Unequalled in power, She was accompanied by Her son, Centeotl, a savior god and fertility sacrifice.[52]

Ixchel of the Mayas was a Moon goddess, deity of childbirth, fertility, lunar cycles, weaving of the fabric of life, and healing. During the rite of passage, young Mayan women traveled to Her temple on the sacred Isle of women. Ixchel is identical to Spider Woman.

The Aztec goddess Xochiquetzal, as Goddess of all women, was a Mexican version of Aphrodite. She was a Mother-Crone figure, but also a Moon virgin, the complete Triple Goddess. She presided over love, marriage, sacred harlots, music, spinning and weaving, magick, art, and changes. She had a son/lover much like Adonis.[53] In mythology, after the primal flood, She brought forth all humanity, speechless until Her sacred dove descended, creating the world's languages.

Coatlicue (the Aztecs called Her Lady of the Serpent Skirt) was the Mother of all Aztec deities, Creatress of all earthly life, and keeper of the dead. Walker says Her skirt may have been made of the penises of Her castrated lovers.

The Primal Mother of the Aztecs was Malinalxochitl, who ruled over all humans and beasts in the beginning. When She was defeated and replaced by Her brother, who became the patriarchal leader of the Aztecs, Malinalxochitl was made into a demon.

Another Aztec goddess of creation was Tlalteutli, whose body was the universe. The Aztec priests spread the tale that She would refuse to bring forth any new life unless She was fed a constant diet of human hearts and blood; thus began the bloody sacrifices of this culture.[54]

Chantico as goddess of the home, fertility, and pleasure was also known as a deity of pain. Chicomecoatl was a maize goddess similar to Demeter. Xilonen was a maize goddess, too. Tozi, or Teteoinnan, was called Mother of the gods, a Nature goddess.

The main Incan goddesses were all of the Mother type: Mama Cocha, Mother Sea; Mama Quilla, the Moon goddess; and Pachamama, Earth Mother.

The faces of the Mother aspect of the Triple Goddess are many. They range from the detached Creatress (a blending with the Maiden aspect) to the totally involved Nurturer to the judgmental, fierce Mother (a blending with the Crone aspect). Each civilization and culture around the world saw the Great Mother in a slightly different way, yet underlying all descriptions was the most vital and important one: the birthing, creating Mother Goddess without whom humanity or anything else would not exist; the throned Queen who guards the treasure of hidden knowledge and prophecy.

If we have learned our lessons of self-examination and seeing the truth from the Maiden, then the Mother welcomes us at the center of the inner labyrinth. It is only with Her omnipotent help that we can face and transform the negativities we have stored within our subconscious minds.

The Mother shows us how to love ourselves, just as we really are, not the masked image we show to others or the phantom image that others have created for us and of us. She makes clear the positive qualities we may have missed or chosen not to see. She also shines Her light on the negatives, encouraging us to transform them into positives. The Mother frowns upon unnatural austerities and mistreatment of bodies and minds, whether our own or those of others of Her creations. Joy of life in every aspect is one of Her commandments—joy with responsibility.

If we are willing to listen and learn at Her feet, the Mother teaches us how to use our inborn gifts of intuition and prophecy. She shows us Her Mysteries of the cycles of our lives, this world, and the universe, and the connection each has with the others. Her knowledge is boundless, for it encompasses the past, the present, and the future. However, these gifts of knowledge come with a price: the acceptance of responsibility for the choices we make and the things we do. There is no way the Mother will let us ignore this law. If we try to avoid this, She will simply bring us back into a similar situation, repeating the cycle until we have no choice but to learn.

The Mother is the Keeper of the treasure, the central point of the spiral or labyrinth. She is, and ever has been, the churning cauldron or matrix of all creation and re-creation deep within the collective unconscious. She is the supreme Divine Teacher, the Initiator, the spiritual High Priestess, the Empress of all levels of body, mind, and spirit. As long as we keep trying to improve and learn from Her, She is infinite patience itself. If we break Her laws, She brings us up short, usually with a painful lesson that we never forget.

Her love for and interest in Her children never ends. The Mother wishes for us only the best and brightest of lives. However, She is aware, as is any mother, that only by finding our own way to Her Divine Center and making our own mistakes can humanity grow in a positive, productive way. We have only to ask for Her aid, and She holds out Her hands in welcome. Sitting at Her feet in the Divine Center, we find calmness, inner peace, and direction in life. The Mother is truly Mother of all.

PART IV
THE CRONE

VIII

THE GODDESS AS CRONE

The Crone aspect of the Great Goddess is the least understood and most feared of the three aspects. She has been called the Terrible Mother, the Hag, the Dark Mother, the Wise One. Because She deals with death and the end of cycles, most people tend to avoid this face of the Goddess. Black is Her color, and sometimes dark blue and the deepest of purples. Black is the absorber of all light, the color of darkness where all life rests before rebirth. The Crone is winter, night, outer space, the abyss, menopause, advancement of age, wisdom, counsel, the gateway to death and reincarnation, and the Initiator into the deepest of Mysteries and prophecies. The waning Moon is Her monthly time of power.

The Crone's number is nine and multiples of nine. This number symbolizes wisdom and sacred magick. Nine is also a Moon number, which means spiritual completion and wholeness. The Moon goes through its phases from New to Waxing to Full and back again to New. In life, we go out from the Crone's recycling cauldron into existence, then eventually return again to Her waiting vessel. Physical death is part of life's cycle of wholeness.

Every living human must come to terms, sooner or later, with the Dark Mother or the Crone aspect of the Goddess. Nearly everyone is afraid of death and old age, some more intensely than others. Ordinarily, this fear of death is a healthy deterrent, keeping us from harming ourselves with unnecessary and dangerous risks. This fear, or will to live, is necessary to keep us fighting for survival, for life when we are ill or depressed.

Everyone ages; there is no such thing as eternal youth. Both men and women go through a stage in life when their hormones decrease and their bodies begin to change. Advanced age and the wisdom of experience that comes with it should be honored and looked forward to with anticipation. It is a time of life when one should look back with introspection, remembering the good times with gladness and the bad times with wisdom. It is ideally a time of rest, release from most of the everyday worries of raising a family and holding down a job.

Older people have so much of interest to be shared. It is a shame that in our society we relegate the older generation to uselessness when the rest of us could benefit from their help and hard-earned knowledge. What is history to us, happened to them. It should be an obligation of the elders of each family to set down the family history—all the accomplishments, trials, even the recurring diseases—so that valuable records are not lost.

It is important during this cycle of life that we do not vegetate, but continue to learn new skills and expand old ones, exercise in whatever way best suits each of us, read, and most of all continue to take part in life. Elders can pass on their knowledge by helping in schools, tutoring programs, and community centers. They should show they are wise, vibrant, caring, and loving. No age is an excuse for discourtesy; respect must be earned by positive actions.

This stage of life is also a period when we should be seriously contemplating our mortality, making sure our path through the inner labyrinth is clear. A comfortable relationship with the Crone, hopefully fostered at an earlier time, will prepare us to handle the loss of friends and family. Eventually, this relationship will help us make our own transition back to Her belly-cauldron in a peaceful fashion. All of these things are excellent reasons to reconnect whatever the age.

However, the Crone aspect of the Goddess goes far beyond the recycling process. The Dark Mother is the ultimate Teacher of the very deepest of spiritual Mysteries. She teaches the wonders and possible dangers of trance; Her Mysteries include the contacting of spirits. It is through Her that we learn to prophesy, seeing clearly backward and forward through time.

The Crone is the Keeper of the Akashic Records, the details of all our past lives. If we do not acknowledge the Crone, how can we "remember ourselves," as Gurdjieff said? Through the Dark Mother and the records of our past lives, we learn the necessity of focusing our energy into important things, such as spiritual growth, living our lives the best we can, and seeking the Goddess within. Energy can be translated as strong impulses. Jung said that physical and psychic energy may well be aspects of the same thing. We should learn to take care how we use both.

The Crone aspect of the Goddess is valuable when we need to end a cycle, a relationship, an on-going problem, or whatever. She closes one cycle so that the Maiden can open another. She is the Great Recycler, pulling in all energy and matter that has reached the end of its time, breaking it down in Her cauldron so that the Maiden can create the matrix seed and the Mother can reform it and re-create.

While the Maiden is the dispassionate guardian of balance, the Crone is the Sorrowing Mother who dispenses justice with both love and sadness. She knows the laws must be upheld, but that does not keep Her from feeling sorrow when the verdict appears harsh to us. Injustice and imbalance, in whatever forms, are anathema to Her. We may not understand or see the balancing of the life scales, but the Crone never rests until those scales are in balance.

The Crone blends with both the Mother and the Maiden, creating a continuous cycle within the Great Goddess Herself. She is the shadow behind the Mother's throne in the Divine Center, the ultimate Prophetess who sees all past, present, and future; the supreme Judge, the Elder of unlimited wisdom. As the Mother knows what She is and the Maiden what She will become, so the Crone knows that She has been and will be.

The Dark Mother never seeks us; we must seek Her. When we have finally reached the Divine Center and sit at the Mother's feet to receive knowledge, the Crone appears and beckons. By following Her on into the black void beyond the Mother, we learn that the labyrinth does not end at the center. Rather, it continues through the collective unconscious, winding past frightening primal images and out again on the other side. By continuing this journey under the guidance of the Crone, we find that the spiral that leads downward once more leads through and upward.

The Dark Mother guides us with Her lantern of ultimate truth and wisdom, not running ahead as does the Maiden, but just before us with a firm, confident step. She teaches us that there are unlimited treasures within treasures. She is the Hermit of the Tarot, the Builder who breaks down and rebuilds, the last Fate who cuts the life thread to its allotted length. She is the key to life, the light within darkness, the Power behind the Mother's throne. With Her aid, our eyes are opened to the deepest of spiritual mysteries, and we gain the knowledge needed to plan a new life, whether that be within the one we are now living or the next life in a long cycle of lives.

The Crone is as important to the existence of the Great Goddess as are the Maiden and the Mother. Their aspects are so merged and intertwined that they cannot truly be separated; one aspect leads automatically into another. The Great Goddess is each of these and all of them.

THE CRONE AND MAGICK

Crone magick has a definite place in the life of humans. It teaches us to fully comprehend the entire cycle of life, from beginnings to endings. The Crone has black, dark blue, or deep purple as Her color. This represents the color of darkness where all life rests before rebirth. This aspect of the Goddess is winter, night, wisdom, counsel, deep mysteries and prophecies, the gateway to death and reincarnation. The waning Moon is Her monthly point of power.

The Crone is honored at the Pagan holidays of Halloween (Samhain) and Winter Solstice. Many Christians still celebrate the day after Halloween as All Saints Day, a day for remembering the dead. The Winter Solstice is shared with the Maiden and the Mother, for that holiday is a special time of the Triple Goddess, the rebirth of the Sacred Child, sometimes called the Sun King.

As with the other two aspects of the Goddess, Crone magick can be used with meditations, candleburning, poppets, and other general rituals. Since the Crone is not a birth goddess, Her magick deals with harvesting and the resting of fields, animals, and humans. Her powers affect the ending of all cycles; knowledge of the deepest of Mysteries and prophecies is in Her domain. Within humans, the Crone is the cyclical slowing down of the physical, the total aging process, the desire for rest from the life's daily activities. The person begins to turn inward, spending more time in contemplation and planning more explicit goals. Priorities change. The frantic pace of the outer world assumes less importance.

Following are examples of rituals that fall within the Crone's domain of power:

1. Ending relationships, jobs, friendships.

2. Menopause, or coming to terms with aging.

3. Divorce.

4. A regrouping of energies needed at the end of a cycle of activity or problem.

5. Rest and calmness before making new goals or plans.

6. When the garden or plants are ready for winter.

7. Harassment of any kind.

8. Retribution on rapists, murderers, abusers.

9. On the death of a person or pet; of any animal or human. Contemplation of the end of your own life cycle.

10. When moving from a dwelling place or job.

11. When strong protection is needed from attacks on the physical or psychic levels, or even annoyance by spirits.

12. To understand the deepest of Mysteries.

13. Developing trance or communication with the guides and other spirits.

The power of the Crone can be summoned with dark shades of candles, such as black,[1] dark blue, or the deepest of purples. If you must call upon Her for protection or retribution, be certain that you are justified in your actions. Even then, it is best not to state what you want to happen. Simply place the problem before the Crone and let Her decide what, if any, penalties will be exacted and how they will occur. Follow the suggestions for candleburning given in the chapters on the Maiden and Mother.

The Crone can be honored during the late fall and winter by arranging gourds and bright autumn leaves in a bowl or cauldron. This is a visual reminder of the turning of the cycles and seasons. At Halloween, it is nice to light a black candle at sunset in remembrance of all your ancestors who have gone before you. Place the candle in a safe place to burn out.

At Winter Solstice, many Pagans burn white, red, and black candles in honor of the Goddess in all Her aspects, but also as a visual reminder that everything is born, is creative, dies, and is born again.

The Crone aspect of the Goddess is the hardest to relate to because of the negative propaganda She has received over the centuries. However, common sense tells us that we all return to Her cauldron. We need to recall that this descent into the cauldron or abyss is only a time of rest and renewal. She should not be dreaded, but welcomed. One good mental exercise to dispel fear is to meditate upon going into Her cauldron-like existence, meeting Her face to face, and feeling the love She bears for all Her creations.

The Crone is not the end of anything, but rather blends once more into the Maiden aspect of rebirth and renewal. There is really no end to the cycle. Like a gigantic wheel of existence, the cycle repeats itself over and over. The dark void of the night sky and outer space are symbols of the Crone. She is the deep power of recycling and re-creation from basic elements. She is the natural end of all cycles, even mental and spiritual. The Crone is our will to rest and be revived, our intuition speaking when a relationship or activity should be ended. She is the balanced destructive-recreative seed within the cells of every creation, whether human, animal, or galactic body.

She is not the fearsome cowled figure bearing a scythe, but rather a loving Goddess who gathers all into Her belly-cauldron to be remade and reborn. We must teach ourselves to once more see Her as She is: not annihilation, pain, and perpetual suffering, but deep love, comfort, and understanding.

IX

WORLD CRONE
MYTHS

The Crone aspect of the Goddess is the third face of the Great Goddess. The Dark Mother is the most deeply hidden, the most difficult to understand, of the Goddess's faces. She is unavoidable Time, the One with whom we must make our peace if we are to really grow in the greatest of spiritual depths.

Jung calls Her the dark side of the human psyche.[1] Sometimes this is called the shadow self, the dark personal "demons" we each have buried in the subconscious mind. Too many times we deny the past events that produced these demons, thus giving them power over our present and future. In order to heal these wounds and exorcise these demons, we need to follow the inner labyrinth to the place where the shadow self dwells. We must develop a relationship with this shadow self, the Dark Mother within, before we can empower ourselves again.

The Crone form of the Goddess is still remembered in such names and words as Scotland, Caledonia, Nova Scotia, chronometer, calendar, Knossos, hell, core, holly, and others. Although this facet of the Great Mother was shoved farthest into the background, humans have kept the Wise One alive in their collective unconscious and subconscious minds. She is an integral part of life.

The Goddess as Crone was known by various titles: Old Woman, Wise One, the Dark Mother, Hag. Budge, in his translation of *The Egyptian Book of the Dead*, writes that the word "hag" may have come from the Egyptian *heq*, meaning a matriarchal ruler who knew magickal words of power. The Greeks called Hecate the Hag of the Dead. The Old Norse *hagi* meant the Iron Wood, a sacred place of sacrifice. Their goddess Angurboda was Hag of the Iron Wood, and Her daughter was Hel.[2] A holdover of this word is found in Scotland where haggis (hag's dish) is made of internal organs. The festival of Hag's Moon, Hagmena, is still kept as New Year's. In Old High German a wise woman was called Hagazussa, or Moon priestess.[3]

In ancient Egypt, a five-lobed shape surrounded by a circle symbolized the Tuat, or underworld.[4] It also stood for Nephthys and Hekat in Egypt, and Ana in the Middle East. A modern version of this circled pentagram can be seen on Wiccan altars, as an emblem of the Element of Earth.

The underworld realm of the Dark Mother or Crone was not originally viewed as only a place of punishment; it was not until Christian domination that hell became a terrible level of unending tortures. The underworld was simply a place of the dead in the beginning. Sometimes this realm was divided into areas for those who had obeyed the laws and merely awaited rebirth and for those who had disobeyed the laws and were receiving what they deserved. Other times, the underworld was seen as a place of all spirits of the dead, regardless of their earthly behavior. But primarily, the realm of the Dark Mother was a stopover and preparation place for rebirth into another physical life.

The cauldron, or dark churning belly-womb, was a widely acknowledged symbol of the Crone aspect of the Goddess. The Hindus knew it as the pot of blood in Kali's hand; the Norse called it the pot of inspirational mead from which Odin stole his powers. In Babylon, Siris, the goddess of fate, stirred the blue cauldron of heaven. The Chaldeans and Hittites both believed in seven heavenly cauldrons and the seven chthonic cauldrons of Mother Death. The Egyptians called the regenerating cauldron the Lake of Fire. In Wales, Branwen owned the Cauldron of Regeneration that revived men overnight. The Irish goddess Badb had a "boiling" pot of life, wisdom, inspiration, and enlightenment.[5] This cauldron later became a chalice or cup, and eventually the Christian Holy Grail.

The Irish sheila-na-gigs have been predominantly viewed as the birthing goddesses. But some of them cannot be interpreted in this manner, for the figures are gaunt and bony, almost corpse-like. This puts them in the category of the Caillech or Crone, the same as the Hindu goddess Kali; the widespread genitals are symbolic of the birth and death functions. The Crone dissolves matter and energy so that it can be reproduced in a more productive form. The birth process is much like death in that it ends one way of existence and begins another.

Alphabets, especially the Sanskrit one, are often tied to the Crone aspect. Kali Ma wears a necklace of skulls about Her throat, and these skulls are inscribed with the fifty letters of the Sanskrit alphabet. The Hindu mythological stories say that Kali called these the *matrika* (mothers) and formed words with these symbols. Any time myths talk of forming words, it means that creation in some form takes place.

The key is a very mystical emblem. It referred to the hidden spiritual symbolism behind the Mystery Religions and other secret spiritual teachings that held knowledge of the afterlife. The Egyptian ankh was a physical symbol of such a key. The Osirian Mysteries said that holy words were keys to heaven and must not be shared with noninitiates. In the Tarot, the Papess (who was changed into the Pope) holds the keys; mythologically, the Papess represented

Siris and the Cauldron

Persephone and other queens of the underworld who guard the final inner gate in the labyrinth.

The curved blades of scythes represent the lunar crescent of the Goddess. The scythe is a symbolic tool of the Crone as She harvests lives. The name came from an ancient Scythian goddess; the Greeks called Her Gaea, Artemis, or Rhea Kronia. The modern Grim Reaper of New Year's was based on the Crone and Her scythe.

Originally, among the Celts in particular, Halloween (or Samhain) was the Feast of the Dead. It is still said among Pagans and others of mystical knowledge that the evening of Samhain finds the veil between worlds the thinnest. Thus it is easier for the deceased to communicate with the living at that time. The Crone, who unfortunately has been turned into a hideous witch, is still honored by this holiday, although one must admit it is a backhanded honor. The "demons" who are supposed to be abroad on this night were originally the priestesses who knew how to directly communicate with the dead; this communication was undoubtedly a source of comfort and information to families.

Chaos, the universe of formless recycled energy and matter, is the working place of the Crone or Wise One. Chaos is also called the Regenerative Womb, the Darkness of the Abyss, the Ocean of Blood. To the

Kali

Egyptians, the Crone, ruler of Chaos, was Temu, who became Tiamat of the Babylonians. The Hindus knew Her as Maha-Kali or Kali Ma.

Today, the best known Crone goddess is Kali Ma of the Hindus. Kali, the Dark Mother, is a Triple Goddess in Herself in one sense. One of the most dramatic of Her images shows Her squatting over the dead Shiva, devouring his penis with Her vagina while physically eating his intestines. To men, this is a particularly difficult image to view in a spiritual way; after all, contemplation of castration is not a pleasant thought.[6] But it was not meant to be taken literally, or visually, on a physical level. In later times, however, the priests of Cybele did take it literally, performing self-castration as part of their dedication to the goddess. Even as far away as Finland, there was a Black Goddess named Kalma, a deity who haunted tombs and was said to eat the dead;[7] the Dakinis of Kali became the European Vilas.

But this statue of Kali, if thought upon as Trinity, has a totally different spiritual meaning. With Her vagina, Kali takes the seed to be recreated within Her eternal womb. She also devours and destroys all life in order for it to be reformed, ready for another cycle of existence. This vivid statue of the Goddess is a visual reminder of Her creation-preservation-destruction abilities.

The Tantric worshippers of Kali realized the importance of facing Her Crone aspect as well as Her re-creative qualities. If one fears one aspect of the Great Goddess, how can one truly understand Her universality? Real wisdom must be total; as with self-realization, one must be willing to know all aspects of wisdom, of reality.

Kali's necklace of skulls was engraved with the Sanskrit letters which were considered the magickal mantras by which She created through combining the Elements.[8] Her worshippers were the first to use the idea of the creative Word or Logos. Usage of magickal mantras or words is still in existence today, particularly among members of Eastern religions and Western Ceremonial Magicians.

Although black is primarily the color of the Crone, Kali in Her three forms had the sacred gunas, which were white, red, and black. These colors representing the Triple Goddess are still used in Wicca and, strangely enough, on certain Christian altars at Christmas.

Kali also had three groups of priestesses who served Her. The Yoginis or Shaktis were the Maidens, the virgin (independent) sexual priestesses; the Matri were the Mothers, the bearers of the god-begotten children;[9] the Dakinis, the Crones, or angels of death of the cremation grounds prepared the dying and their families for the transition and upon their own death were said to become the guides into the land of the dead.[10] The Tantric yogis and the Dakinis worship Her in the cremation grounds as Smashana-Kali. Although ritual killing is greatly lessened in India today, originally Kali was given bloody sacrifices of male animals;[11] no female animals were allowed to be slain and offered to Her, for She is the Female Principle.

Today, Kali is primarily known as Dakshinakali, the south-facing black Kali.[12] She is usually shown as black and naked; She is full-breasted with dishevelled hair and wild grimaces on Her face. Around Her waist is a girdle of human hands, a symbol of karma and the deeds of life. Her three eyes are the past, present, and future. Generally, Kali has four hands, symbolic of the blending of male and female principles, but on occasion She is shown with as few as two or as many as eight. Her left hands hold a severed head and sword while the right ones gesture signs of dispelling fear and encouraging spiritual strength. Like Her husband Shiva, Kali dances the cosmic dance of creating, for within Her combine and blend all cosmic forces and energies. Some of Her images show Her in a dancing position surrounded by flames, the creative fire. Kali Ma is also Time, its continuing cycles of beginning-ending-beginning.

The Crone aspect of another trinity of Hindu goddesses was Uma. She is also known as Prisni, mother of the demons Maruts and Rudras. In most of Her forms, particularly the one with the vagina dentata, Uma is quite clearly Mother Death, the Dark Mother.

Nekhbet, the very old Egyptian name for Mut, was the vulture goddess of death and rebirth. The vulture, as eater of the dead, was one of the oldest animal totems belonging to the Great Goddess in Egypt. There was even a Stele of the Vultures in ancient Catal Huyuk, from the seventh millennium BCE. Along with the serpent goddess Buto, the vulture deity Nekhbet was one of two Mistresses who were considered guardians of the royal dynasties and nurturers of the deceased pharaohs. Temples had special chapels in the west for Nekhbet, where daily She awaited the dying Sun.

The original City of the Dead, Nekhen, held one of Egypt's oldest oracular shrines to this goddess.[13] Since this was both a birth and death shrine, the Greeks identified Nekhbet with Aphrodite Ilithyia. The Romans named it after Juno Lucina, the goddess of childbirth.[14]

In hieroglyphics, the sign for mother was a vulture. On mummy pillows She was pictured holding an ankh, the key of life, in each claw. The Egyptian Book of the Dead says that the first gate of the underworld was guarded by Nekhbet.

Nephthys, the Revealer and wife of Set, was an underworl
Sometimes She was pictured with winged arms. With Isis, Her si
was known as the Two Ladies, symbolizing life and death. Neph.
very similar to Hecate.

Although Nephthys was the wife of the evil Set, She had no children until She lay with Her brother Osiris. From this union came the
strange child Anubis with black skin and the head of a jackal. In fear of
what Set would do, Nephthys abandoned the baby to Isis who raised him.
When Set later, in a bid for supreme power, killed and dismembered
Osiris, Nephthys left him. Thereafter, Nephthys and Isis worked together.

Nephthys is the loving Crone, the Dark Mother within the collective unconscious and subconscious minds, who knows that children
(ideas) cannot be born from sterility (Set); they must come from life
(Osiris) and participation in life. After these ideas become formed in the
subconscious, they are born or released into the conscious mind. Only
then can they grow and become useful, as Anubis grew under the loving
care of Isis (life) and learned the magick of embalming. Embalming is the
preservation of something. In a spiritual sense, embalming is the preservation and solidification of an idea in a permanent form. The sterility of
negative thoughts causes fragmentation of positive thoughts and ideas;
they create chaos in life plans and activities, leaving a person in a constant state of indecision and inaction (death). Only when the Crone
within joins with the Mother within can true accomplishment be made.

Ament, or Amenti, known as the Westerner, was another Egyptian
goddess of the underworld. Her symbols were the hawk and a feather.

Sekhmet, or Sekhet,[15] the lion-headed goddess, was the destroying
power of sunlight. She could direct "fire" from a great distance to destroy
the enemies of Osiris. She always protected the good and destroyed the
evil. In a variant form as Mehenet the serpent goddess, Sekhmet stood on
the head of Ra and shot fiery darts at the god's enemies.

Tefnut was fed on the blood of the dead. A very primitive Egyptian
goddess, She was said to live at the bottom of the underworld and was a
balance and twin of Nut, who lived at the top of the sky. A group of
underworld demon-gods hacked apart the dead in order to feed Tefnut
the blood—perhaps a reminder of Neolithic human sacrifices. She was
always red and in many ways resembled Kali Ma.

There were several Crone goddesses in the Middle East, one of
whom was Tiamat. She was considered the goddess of the primal abyss,
the Creatress and Destroyer. In Egypt, Tiamat was known as Temu or Te-
Mut; sometimes She was called Ma-Nu, the great fish who birthed all

creation and periodically reswallowed everything.[16] Her consort Apsu was not Her equal or even, according to myth, necessary. Her menstrual blood, which flowed for three years and three months, was said to be held in the reservoir of the Red Sea.

Tiamat was considered the fertile tumultuous sea in the Epic of Creation. She and Her consort Apsu created the celestial world and the gods. These lesser deities, the Igigi and the Anunnaki, were so exuberant in their activities that Apsu went to Tiamat with the suggestion of getting rid of them. The Goddess refused. But Ea, leader of those deities, found out about Apsu's proposed annihilation. The lesser deities retaliated by sending Marduk against Tiamat.[17] By slaying his mother, Marduk made himself king of the gods and created the heavens and Earth out of Her split body.

Tiamat is the Crone with Her regenerative cauldron. As the Divine Feminine, She has no desire to destroy Her creations; however, the Divine Masculine often points out the dangers of letting humans run amuck, disturbing the balance of the universe. We each have within us the Divine Feminine and Masculine, the caring and the warning parts of our collective unconscious minds. If we are not realistic in weeding out the negatives in our lives, we may end up being destroyed. Sometimes, like Tiamat in the myth, we wait too long to take action and must pay the penalties. What we say we love is not always good for us. Often we must make a painful choice.

Ereshkigal, dark sister of Ishtar, was queen of the underworld, actually seven hells. She is similar to Nephthys, Persephone, Kali, and Hel. Her consort Nergal was a much later addition to the myths. Ereshkigal, sometimes called Allatu, was helped by the 600 Anunnaki, or demon spirits.[18]

To the Assyrians of Nineveh and Arbela, Ishtar, as Lady of Battles, was the daughter of the god Sin and the sister of the Sun god Shamash. She went into battle standing on a chariot pulled by seven lions; in Her hands She held a mighty bow. In this aspect, Ishtar was said to create dissension as the Star of Lamentation.

Not much is known about the goddess Gula, except that She inflicted illness or restored health. Known as the Lady of Birth and Mother of Dogs, this Babylonian goddess also ruled fate.[19]

In Greece, Circe was a Crone Moon goddess, the Fate-Spinner. One of Her symbols was the cauldron. She was called upon for vengeance, physical love, and dark magick. Homer called Her a witch who turned men into swine. Circe was associated with the death-bird kirkos, or the

falcon; the isle of Aeaea was a funerary shrine to Her. Her name is connected with the circle, or cirque; this shows Her to be identified with the
fate spinners.[20] Homer wrote of Her as Circe of the Braided Tresses,
pointing to the ancient belief in priestesses' power through magickal
knowledge of knots and braids.

The patriarchal Greeks said that Circe poisoned Her husband, the
king of the Sarmatians, and went to live on Aeaea where She built a
beautiful palace. She used magick potions to turn all men who landed
there into swine. The only exception was Odysseus who was protected by
the magick herb moly, given to him by Hermes.

It is quite possible that originally a priestess of this goddess was
forced to marry the mentioned king, found the situation impossible, did
poison him, and went to the island. Since Circe is connected with sexual
rites, any men who went there and participated in the open sexualness
would be thought to be under a spell. Patriarchy looked upon the sacred
sexual rituals as releasing the animal instincts and wallowing in the physical senses, something they abhorred and fought against.

On a spiritual level, this myth has another meaning. The feminine
portion of humans must learn how to break free of stereotypes, flee to the
Mother within, and build there a sacred place of safety in the center of the
labyrinth. Anyone with the old stereotypes within their personality who
comes within the life circle of this centered person will be "charmed" and
under control like a domestic animal. By being under control, I mean that
they would no longer threaten. The only ones who would avoid this
"charming" would be the ones who, through the power of enlightened
thought (the moly and Hermes), presented no threat of any kind.

Cybele, who came to Greece and Rome from Phrygia, was both a
Crone and Mother goddess. According to mythology, Cybele was both the
grandmother and lover of the handsome youth Attis. With his handsome
face and body, Attis had no trouble finding many females who succumbed
to his charms. Cybele's jealous rage drove the young man insane; he castrated himself in remorse and died. The death and rebirth of Attis formed
the central portion of Cybele's Mysteries. The priests of this goddess castrated themselves in wild rituals. This Mystery-Religion based on Cybele
was similar in many respects to those of Demeter and Hecate.[21] Long
before the advent of the Sun god Mithras, Cybele was honored by the sacrifices of bulls and the baptizing of Her followers in the blood.

The Crone is patient only so long with those who claim to give Her
honor and then go off in other directions. Ignoring Her, denigrating Her,
disbelieving in Her—all these do not affect the Crone's existence, but

they certainly cause problems for us. We become unbalanced (insane). We make ourselves impotent in life. When we finally face death, we are afraid and remorseful, wishing we had done things differently. But the Crone in Her wisdom and jealous love for humanity will recycle us in Her cauldron, and we will be reborn.

Hecate of the Amazons was a Moon and underworld deity. Her chariot was often shown pulled by dragons. She was the oldest Greek form of the triform Goddess, who ruled heaven, the underworld, and the Earth. After the matriarchs fell, the Greeks worshipped Hecate only as queen of the underworld and ruler of three-way crossroads. As Hecate Trevia, Hecate of the Three Waπys, Her images stood at these crossroads where offerings of dogs, honey, and black ewe lambs were left on Full Moon nights. Divination and communication with the dead were performed in these places.[22]

She was also known as *angelos* (angel) and *phosphoros* (light). In the myth of Kore-Persephone, Hecate does not interfere when the Maiden is dragged down into the underworld. Demeter is outraged and vengeful, but Hecate remains calm, knowing that certain things in life must come to pass and there is little point in becoming hysterical about them. This inner illumination (phosphoros) of consciousness, this learning to roll with the punches and then coming back to better things, is the deep wisdom taught by the Dark Mother, the dark angel (angelos) of the collective unconscious. If we do not know this aspect of the Goddess or acknowledge Her wisdom, we cannot have a truly integrated personality.

Later statues show Hecate with three heads and six arms, or merely as a pillar called a Hecterion. Hecate was shown holding three torches, a key, a rope, and a dagger. With the key She unlocks the deep Mysteries; the rope is either a scourge or a symbolic umbilical cord; the dagger, which has become the athame of Wicca, cuts through illusion to true power.[23] But Hecate was also known as the "most lovely one," a name for the Moon. It was said that She wore a shimmering headdress and was second to none in powers of sorcery.

A statue from the eighth century BCE shows Hecate with wings and holding a snake. Hecate was called the Silver-Footed Queen of the Night, as was Persephone.[24] In Italy at Lake Averno, an extinct volcanic crater, the thick, dark forest surrounding the lake was known as Hecate's sacred grove.[25] Actual temples to this goddess were rare. During the Middle Ages, Hecate became known as Queen of the Witches.

Persephone, who was Kore before She went to the underworld, was known as Queen of the Dead or Hell. Two of Her emblems were the bat and the pomegranate. The Romans called Her Proserpina. This goddess was much older than the Eleusinian Mysteries which honored Her and Demeter. Her Etruscan name was Persipnei. The Orphic mystics said She held the keys to heaven and hell (Elysium and Tartarus). Her story is told in the chapter on the Maiden.

Many of the Goddess myths of Africa have been lost. We do know of a few Crone goddesses, among them Asase Yaa (who both created life and received the dead) and Ala (Ale, Ane), who was queen of the dead and the harvest.

In the Celtic cultures, Arianrhod of Wales was sometimes viewed as the Crone, although She was also a Mother aspect of the Goddess. Although Arianrhod was a star and sky goddess, She dealt with reincarnation and death. Her Silver Wheel was a symbol of the karmic wheel, the endless circling of time. This wheel was also known as the Oar Wheel, a ship which carried dead warriors to Her realm. Her palace of Caer Arianrhod, or the Aurora Borealis, was sometimes referred to as Emania, or Moon-land of the dead.

Caillech was the Crone, particularly in Scotland. A derivative of Her name, Caledonia, was given to that country. Her name, as well as Her title as Black Mother, is too close to the name Kalika, a title of Kali, to be coincidence. Graves, in

Caillech

Morgan Le Fay

The White Goddess, says the Caillech was another form of Scathach and Skadi. The people knew Her as a spirit of disease; in Ireland, She was prayed to by sufferers of smallpox.[26] Caillech means either an old woman, a hag, or a veiled one. The veiled image relates Her to the mysteries of knowing the future, particularly the time of one's death. Medieval legend turned Her into the Black Queen of a western paradise, the one Spaniards called Califia; the word California comes from this.

Scathach or Scota was another Crone of both Ireland and Scotland. She was called the Destroyer of the underworld. A death goddess, She was very similar to both the Caillech and Skadi of the Norse-Germanic clans.

Cerridwen was the great Crone of Wales. She was connected with the Moon, the cauldron, and grain. The white, corpse-eating sow, representing the Moon, was one of Her animal emblems. The great Welsh bard Taliesin claimed to be born of Her. In fact, the Welsh bards as a group called themselves *cerddorion*, sons of Cerridwen. Communing with Her and being given a drink from Her magickal cauldron was said to confer the greatest inspiration for poets and musicians.

In Ireland, Macha of the Goddess Trinity was Mother Death. Her primary functions had to do with war and death. Macha was actually worshipped in Ireland before the coming of the Celts. Her famous shrine was Emain Macha, capital of Ulster.[27] She liked to haunt battlefields and did magick with the blood of the slain men.[28] The origin of the banshee may come from this goddess, for some say that Her voice summons men to death;[29] the banshee was not always a figure of terror, for she gave warnings and gently took others into death.

The Morrigan, who was triple in Herself and often called the Three Morrigans, was a dark Death Goddess. She was known throughout Ireland, Wales, and Britain. In Munster, Ireland, She was known as Mugain. One of Her animal symbols was the raven that haunted the battlefields.

Just before the great battle between the Tuatha de Danaan and the Fomorians, the Dagda was reconnoitering. He met the Morrigan bathing in a river. She promised him victory in battle if he copulated with Her, which he did. The Dagda is the Celtic god of Earth and magick. The Morrigan was the goddess of battles, although She never participated directly. The copulating of these two areas of energy represents action and physical activity influenced by spiritual power. Victory in any project (physical, mental, emotional, spiritual) comes only when one is able to recognize opportunity and take the initiative while applying physical, magickal, and spiritual laws; these laws are all interconnected and are best used in cooperation with each other.

In the Arthurian romances, this goddess became Morgan Le Fay, the witch or sorceress. On Gawain's blood-red shield was painted Her pentacle. The old Welsh word for witches' spells was *glamor*; this came from Glamorgan, Her sacred territory.

The Norse-Germanic cultures had several Crone goddesses. Hel, queen of the dead and the underworld, has been given the most description in the writings. Although Hel was a terrible creature to look at and in the patriarchal myths would side against the gods and humans at Ragnarok, She received all of the dead, except those who died in battle. Walker writes that the expression *Hella cunni* (Hel's kinsmen) was later corrupted into Harlequin. During medieval times, the Hellequins, or ladies of the night, went from house to house among the commoners and received food and drink in return for good luck wishes. Perhaps these were remnants of Pagan priestesses. Whatever the Christian church thought of Hel, the common folk generally considered Her more benevolent than harmful.[30]

Hel, the daughter of Loki, was given Her underworld realm by Odin. This realm and Her great palace there were not a place of fear, as the Christians later made it, but simply an abode of the dead. Even the gods eventually went to Hel's realm, as did Balder.

The earliest shrines to Hel were probably uterine-like caves connected with rebirth; these caves may have had some sort of underground volcanic activity or steam vent, thus making a further association of volcanoes with the underworld, or they may have been the containers of ice that were associated with Hel's icy realm. Medieval legends speak of Brynhild (Burning Hel) as a leader of the Valkyries; since the Valkyrie's castle was surrounded by magickal fire through which heroes had to go, this points to a connection with the original goddess Hel. Another of Her names was Nehellania, or Nether Moon, a direct linkage with Nef-Hel, Nifl, or Niflheim, the name of Her underworld kingdom.

Among the North Germanic tribes, She was called Holda or Bertha and rode with Odin in the Wild Hunt.[31] Even in the tenth century, Witchcraft tracts said that Pagan women rode under Her leadership in wild night rides. Holly was sacred to Her, and the Germanic followers of this goddess often made magick wands from its wood. The medieval Christmas carol about holly, which is still sung, and holly's use in decorations at that seasonal holiday show that some of the old Goddess traditions are still in effect today.

Skadi was the goddess of the dark, cruel North with its ice and snow; She was called upon during dark magick. Walker says that Her name was the root of the Gothic *skadus*, which means shadow or shade.[32] Scandinavia was once called Scadin-auja, or the land of Skadi.[33] Each year sacrifices of male blood were made to Skadi, thus linking the Dark Goddess with the re-creating Spring Maiden of renewed growth. The myth of the strange performance of this goddess and Loki is symbolically the first of these sacrifices. The Scandinavian *skalds*, who were poet-shamans, said their powers and inspirations, as well as their name, came from the Dark Mother Skadi. It was believed that whatever they prophesied came true because they had a direct connection with the only valid source, the cauldron of all time within the realm of the Crone.

Norse myth describes Skadi as the beautiful daughter of the Giant Thjazi. After Her father was killed by Thorr, She came to the gates of Asgard and challenged the gods. In an attempt to dissipate Her anger, Loki (who had cause the problem in the first place) took a goat and went out to greet Her. He tied one end of a rope to the goat and the other to his genitals; the goat pulled one way, Loki the other, until the genitals tore free. Loki fell bleeding into the lap of Skadi, bathing Her loins with his blood. Although Loki was castrated, it must not have been permanent for he went on to pursue other female deities.

When one learns from the Crone with patience and love, one learns that She is not an ugly hag, but a beautiful goddess. One must be willing to "sacrifice" oneself on the inner altar in order to gain Her good will. This type of sacrifice does not literally mean immolation or austerity of unnatural kinds. This is a spiritual sacrifice: willingness to give up negative habits and friends; taking time for meditation and ritual; being open to new ways of spiritual thought and understanding. The only thing we have of value to offer the Dark Mother is the life force of our being. When we can offer ourselves without reservation, the Crone gives in return far more than we can imagine. Like Loki, we lose nothing; what we gain is up to our intentions.

Even the lovely Freyja, basically a Mother goddess, had Her dark side. To Her belonged half of all the slain on a battle-field. These warriors were taken to Her Marsh-Halls and the Folkvangr, the Field of War-riors.[34] When the gods and

Skadi

Vila

men pushed Her too far, when they forgot the principles of justice, honor, and peace, Freyja became the Destroying Crone who balanced out life.

In the Eddas, Angurboda was the mother of Hel and the Moondogs who took away the dead. Although She is described as a hag, this means "Holy One."[35]

The ruler and queen of the Lapp underworld was Yambe-Akka. Baba-Yaga was queen of the dead in the Slavonic-Russian cultures. The Finnish-Ugric queen of the underworld, or land of the dead, was Tuonetar, the queen of Tuonela.

Mara, the death-bringing Crone goddess, was known in one form or another among many of the Indo-European clans. The Slavs said that Mara or Mora drank the blood of men at night. Like Kali squatting over Shiva, they said that She was the Nightmare that squatted on the chest and crushed the breath from the body.

The Slavonic Vilas (mentioned earlier) were spirits associated with water and the Crone; the Russian equivalent were the Rusalki. It is possible that the word Vila is related to the Scandinavian Vala and Valkyrie. Later, Vilas or Wilas came to mean the dangerous souls of drowned women who enticed humans to join them.

In ancient China, Chih Nii, or Chih Nu, was called the goddess of spinners. Meng-Po Niang-Niang was the goddess of hell and reincarnation. Lady Meng was said to live in a house just inside the exit from Hell; there She brewed the special Broth of Oblivion which kept each reincarnating person from remembering his or her past lives.

Tibet had a Crone goddess similar to Durga; Her name was Lha-mo, sometimes known as dMagzor Rgyal-mo. She was known as the Great Queen, the she-devil, and was similar to the Hindu Durga.

Although the people of the Pacific Ocean cultures had no Maiden goddesses, they had several female Crone deities. Biliku of Micronesia sometimes took a spider form; She was known as both kind and terrible. Eingana of Australia was called the Death Mother. In Polynesia, there were Hina (Hine) of darkness and death, Mahui-ike of the underworld, and Miru of the underworld. In Hawaii, Hikuleo was goddess of the underworld, as was Pele; Pele also ruled over volcanoes.

Native American Crone goddesses tended to blend with either the Maiden or the Mother aspects. Iyatiku of the Pueblo was a corn goddess who lived in the underworld. Onatha of the Iroquois was similar to Persephone. As the temperamental goddess of hunting, the sea, and sorcery, Sedna of the Inuit (Eskimo) was both revered and feared.

The Mayas had two Crone goddesses. Ixtab, a blend of Mother and Crone, was the deity of hunting and hanging. Masaya was the death aspect and goddess of volcanoes.

Among the Aztecs, Chalchihuitlicue, goddess of storms and spring, and Xilonen, the maize goddess, were blended with other Goddess aspects. However, Xochiquetzal was known only as goddess of the underworld. This is somewhat confusing as Mictanchihuatl was also considered co-ruler of the nine underground rivers and the souls of the dead.

Tlazolteotl of the Aztecs, whose name can be translated as "lady of filth" or "dirty lady,"[36] rode a broomstick through the night skies, wore a peaked hat, and was associated with the Moon, the snake, and the bat. Like Hecate, much of Her worship was performed at crossroads. The Aztecs were fanatic about what they called unclean behavior or sin, especially sexual sin; the priests of this goddess could grant purification of all sins but only once in a lifetime. This goddess's remission of sins were a prerequisite for the penitent to face the god Tezcatlipoca.[37] The Ciuateteo (right honorable mothers) were Her priestesses; they were said to fly through the air (astral travel?) and were connected with childbirth. Tlazolteotl was connected with Witchcraft, sexuality, gambling,

Tlazolteotl

temptation, and black magick. She had four facets which were recognized as separate goddesses: Tiacapan, Teicu, Tlaco, and Xocutxin.

The Dark Mother or Crone is not to be feared. She is the only one who can peacefully lead each human through the veil between life and death, for She is the Door Keeper of this realm. By seeking, learning from, and attempting to understand the Crone, we prepare for our own easy passage from this life back to Her re-creative cauldron, and once again through the birthing door into another life. This can be understood on more than a physical level. This death, rest, and rebirth applies to cycles within life, to growth from totally physically oriented ways to spiritual development.

The Crone is the Power behind the Throned Queen, the Mother. She is the ultimate Advisor, for She sees clearly back into the past through the present and on into the future. The Crone is the Keeper of the Key to the Akashic Records. The final mysteries of life and the universe are Hers. She is the gentle Death Priestess who meets us at the end of our lives and guides us into the world of spirit.

The Crone blends with the Maiden and Mother as they blend with Her. She is the greatest of Teachers and Initiators, for She leads us downward into the center of the labyrinth web. From that point we have no choice but to face the cycle of life and death; we are shown past lives, the mistakes, the victories, the talents gained. Only when we can accept and understand, at least in part, does the Crone show us the most sacred of Her Mysteries: that the labyrinth does not end but continues on, back into life after life, a never-ending cycle of existence.

PART V
OTHER SACRED THREES
AND MULTIPLES

X

THE FATES AND
OTHER THREES

There are a great many triads of goddesses mentioned in the world's mythologies, but these are not always conveniently divided into the clear aspects of Maiden, Mother, and Crone. However, they are important. Sometimes these goddesses portray a single aspect in all their behaviors; sometimes they are vague remnants of the Triple Goddess. The very fact that they were worshipped and their names still remembered are clues to their importance in spiritual mysteries.

The Greek Fates (portions, shares), although most often spoken of as a triad, also included in a peripheral sense Ilithyia, goddess of childbirth, and Nemesis the Inevitable. The Fates were also called the Moerae (Part), and became known as the Parcae during the Middle Ages. These three serious daughters of Nyx, or Night, were Clotho, Lachesis, and Atropos, the deities who were responsible for the life-thread of destiny of each human. Ilithyia helped the birth of a child, determining the length and pain of labor. Then Clotho began to spin the life-thread;[1] it was up to Her to include certain amounts of happiness, love, success, and failure—everything that makes up life. Her sister Lachesis was the one who measured the life-thread against Her rod, assigned the destiny, and added a portion of luck. But brooding Atropos with Her shears could cut that thread at any time without warning. Not even Zeus could go against a decree by the Moerae.[2]

Three rings were used in special rituals to invoke the Fates well into medieval times.[3] The three gunas, or colored threads, of India were said to run through every life as ordained by Fate; these colors were white, red, and black. Ovid, Theocritus, and others wrote of the same colored life-threads.

Nemesis was the only one who could influence Atropos to let the thread spin into a longer length. Nemesis, the daughter of Eris (strife), was a goddess of punishment for those who broke the laws of life. In Rhamnus in Attica, Nemesis was known as Adrasteia (the Inescapable One) and Rhamnusia; here was Her principal center where She was worshipped along with Themis. Annual festivals, called Nemesia, were held in Athens and Smyrna. A statue of this beautiful goddess wearing a silver crown with stag horns was placed beside the bench of the judges.[4]

She carried out the righteous anger and vengeance of the gods; this was especially true concerning those who were proud, insolent, and egotistical. She was said to right every wrong, track every wrong act to the perpetrator, take luck away from the unworthy, and in general keep humans honest and law-abiding. As the terror of evil-doers, Nemesis had three assistants: Dike, Poena, and Erinys. Some of Her emblems were a wheel, a balance scales, bridle, yoke, rudder, sword, and an apple branch. Nemesis was a balance to the goddess Tyche, who tended to bestow gifts where they were not deserved.[5] It is possible that Nimue in the story of Merlin was derived from this goddess.

The Pythagoreans had a triad of Fates: Heimarmene, Ananke, and Dike. This designation was a philosophical view of the Triple Goddess.

The Greeks also had the Meliae, Ash-Tree Nymphs, who were three mystic Fates.

The Greek Charities were three daughters of Zeus by Eurynome, the daughter of Oceanus. From very early times they were worshipped at Orchomenos[6] in Boeotia and in Sparta, Athens, and Crete, particularly with games and contests. Their names were Euphrosyne (Heart's Joy), Aglaia (Brilliant), and Thalia (Flowering). In the city of Athens there were only two Charities: Kleta and Phaenna; in Athens, Auxo and Hegemone.[7] Annual festivals called the Charitesia were held in their honor; there were contests of games, music, and dances. There were many Grecian temples and groups of statues dedicated to the Charities.

At first they were portrayed as draped figures; later as nude and dancing. It was said that they presided over banquets, dancing, and all social pleasures. They represented gracefulness, beauty, and cheerfulness in Nature and in humans. They assisted both Athene and Hermes. They were called upon when taking an oath and the first cup of wine at banquets was offered to them. Some of their emblems were the rose, myrtle, dice, apples, perfume vases, ears of corn, poppies, the lyre, flute, and syrinx.

In medieval times, the Greek Charities became the Three Graces. They were portrayed in paintings as three nude women dancing. Their names, by this time, had been changed to Voluptas, Castitas, and Pulchritudo, or Laetitia Uberima, Viriditas, and Splendor.

Among the Greek chthonic Mystery centers were the Cabirian Mysteries of the island of Samothrace. During an early period of these rituals, three Cabirian Nymphs were worshipped there; they were the daughters of Hephaestus, who was connected with these Mysteries. Much later these Nymphs were replaced by three minor male deities, sometimes called the Casmilus.

The Roman goddess Fortuna was sometimes singular, but more often known as the Triple Goddess Fata Scribunda (the Fate Who Writes). This triad of deities was concerned with luck and good fortune. Fortuna was a particular favorite of military men, gladiators, and gamblers. As a singular goddess, She was honored in both the soldiers' bathhouse and in the nearby amphitheater at Caerleon in southern Wales[8] by small statues. The name Fortuna may have come from Vortumna, the Great Mother who turns the karmic wheel of fate.[9] Her fate wheel became the Wheel of Fortune on the Tarot cards, and She was renamed Lady Luck.

Although only one Gorgon, Medusa (Cunning One or Queen), was prominent in the myths, two others were mentioned: Stheno (Mighty One) and Euryale (Wandering One). Some Greek patriarchal myths say that Medusa was mortal, a priestess of Athene at one time who profaned the temple by copulating with Poseidon there, while remnants of the earliest stories say these females were once beautiful golden sea goddesses. Stheno and Euryale were never considered to be mortal in any way. Medusa was killed by Perseus who gave Her head to Athene to mount on Her shield.[10]

Gorgons had the bodies of women but their hair was a mass of coiling serpents; it was said that to look into their eyes would turn a person to stone, or bring icy death. The idea of the evil eye may have originated with the Gorgons' petrifying gaze. Like other images of the Terrible Mother around the world, the Gorgons had protruding tongues, huge teeth, glaring eyes, wings, and claws. It was believed that to own a representation of the Gorgon's face was to possess a charm against all negatives.[11] When a person is in a fighting fury, it is possible to see a replica of the Gorgon's face overlaid upon the human one.[12] Robert Graves writes that the frightening, hideous face of Medusa or the Gorgon was originally a sacred mask worn by the priestesses to frighten away any uninitiated people who might try to attend or spy upon the rites.[13]

The Furies, or Erinyes (the Angry Ones), were Alecto (Never-ending, the Unnameable), Tisiphone (Retaliation-Destruction), and Megaera (Envious Anger, Grudge). They were particularly associated with the goddess Demeter in Her chthonic attributes.[14] Other names for these goddesses were the Dirae, Eumenides, and Semnae. Hesiod said they were born from the blood of Uranus; Aeschylus listed them as the daughters of Nyx, calling them Children of Eternal Night; Sophocles wrote that they were the children of Cronus and Eurynome, Daughters of Earth and Shadow.

At first they were portrayed as evil-looking black females, dressed in black drapery, winged, and carrying serpents, knives, and torches. Poisonous blood was said to drip from their eyes. In later times, when they began to be called the Eumenides, they were seen as beautiful but serious maidens who dressed like Artemis. The Greeks called them by the name Eumenides (the Kindly Ones) because they were afraid to use their other name; this new superimposed image did not, however, change their stinging and avenging fury.

Serpent-crowned like the Gorgons, the Furies harried all those who escaped from or defied public justice, natural laws, or those who shed family blood or broke oaths. As attendants of Persephone, they waited at the entrance of the underworld to punish those who died without atonement for their evil deeds. They also harassed living offenders until they were filled with remorse. They were pitiless against those who committed the crime of matricide.[15] The Furies avenged any mother who was insulted, harmed, or murdered by rising out of Hades with a terrifying barking; their punishment was primarily aimed at harassing the perpetrator to the point of madness and death.

The Gorgons and the Furies (Erinyes) are deities tied to the attributes of the Terrible or Dark Mother. By the time that Athene came to be honored by the Greeks, those clans had ceased giving any worship to the Crone and considered Her and any deities representing Her their enemies.[16] Through the intervention of the goddess Athene the Furies were considered subdued, as were the Gorgons when Medusa's head was placed on Athene's shield.

The Harpies were the children of the Titan Thaumas, who was a son of Pontus and Gaea. They had the heads of young women and the bodies, wings, and claws of vicious birds; Walker says they had the bodies of vultures or carrion eaters. The Harpies were named Aello, Okypete, and Celaeno or Podrage. They were used by the higher gods to punish those who broke laws.

The Graeae, or Gray Ones, were three hideous old women who shared one eye and one tooth. They were the offspring of Phorcys and Ceto. Their names were Deino (Alarm, Terror), Pemphredo (Dread, Wasp), and Enyo (Horror, Warlike One). As guardians of the Gorgons, they lived in a dark, dank cave at the entrance to Tartarus. To the Greeks, the Graeae were less terrible than the Gorgons. Their name means the mothers of Greece (Graecia).

The Sirens were deities of the sea and death. Their sweet singing was said to be irresistible to seafarers; because they tended to dwell on rocky, dangerous shores, they lured men and ships to destruction. The names commonly given for them were Parthenope, Ligeia, and Leukosia.

The Horae were the daughters of Zeus and Themis. They represented the seasons of the year; that is, spring, summer, and autumn. Winter, however, was not considered a season because it belonged to the attributes of sleep and death; on the rare occasions when the Horae of winter was pictured, She was nameless. In Athens, only Thallo (Spring) and Karpo (Autumn) were honored, although in all other parts of Greece all three Horae, under different names, were worshipped. Most commonly, their names are given as Eunomia (Wise Legislation), Dike[17] (Justice), and Eirene (Peace). They ruled over order, propriety, and morality in human life. Sometimes the Horae accompanied the Charities and Aphrodite, sometimes the Muses and Apollo.

The worship of Eunomia was never neglected by the Senate since She dealt primarily with political life. Dike reported directly to Zeus of every injustice to any human; Dike's darker side was retribution, or Nemesis.[18] Eirene was the goddess of songs and festivities and was also considered the mother of Plutos, the god of riches who accompanied Dionysus. Sometimes Chloris, a separate goddess of spring who corresponded to the Roman Flora, was worshipped as an Horae. As wife of Zephyros, the West wind, Chloris was a deity of buds and flowers.

Desert Moon Goddesses

The Hesperides was the name of the garden where Hera kept Her golden apples, but it was also the title of three goddesses. At first this triad watched over this garden but, when they could not resist the golden fruit, they were replaced by the serpent Ladon. The Hesperides were the daughters of Atlas the giant and Hesperis, goddess of the West. Their names were Aegle, Erytheis, and Hespere; four more were added at a later date.[19]

The Greek Thriae were connected with Delphi when it was pre-patriarchal and under the control of the Pythia or Pythoness.[20] They were a triad known as the Triple Muse of Divination whose mystery center, the Corycian Cave, was high on the side of Mount Parnassus. It is thought that this cave was the original oracle spot before Delphi was established. These sisters, named Korykia, Daphnis, and Thuia, taught the god Hermes to predict the future by gazing at pebbles in a bowl of water. Their ability to prophesy through a dream state was later taken over by the Delphic oracle. Their symbols were the bee and honey; honey had to be offered before divination was done.

The Augralids were pre-Hellenic goddesses who ruled

the area around Athens before Athene rose to a place of prominence. These goddesses were named Agraulos, Herse, and Pandrosos. An ancient myth, which tells how they broke the trust of a box given into their keeping by Athene, was later changed into the story of Pandora's box. They were basically Earth deities who were replaced by Athene.

There were also three daughters of the Moon in Greek mythology, actually a female trinity. They were Pandia, Erse, and Nemea, and represented the phases of the Moon.

Before patriarchy and the Moslem religion rose to power in Arabia in the seventh century, the people worshipped a triad of desert Moon goddesses: Al-Uzza, Al-Lat, and Manat. Al-Uzza (the Mighty) was a Virgin warrioress of the morning star. Her sacred grove of acacia trees once stood just south of Mecca; in Mecca itself, this goddess was worshipped in the form of a black stone.[21] Al-Lat (Goddess) was an Earth Mother; She was represented by a huge uncut block of white granite in the village of At Ta'if[22] near Mecca. Manat, who corresponds to the Crone, ruled over death and fate. On the road between Mecca and Medina was a large uncut black stone which was worshipped as Her image.

Norns

There was also a trio of Fate goddesses, known as the Norns, among the Norse-Germanic clans. These were named Urd (the Past), Verthandi or Verdandi (the Present), and Skuld (the Future).[23] Sometimes the definitions of their names were given as Become, Becoming, and Shall Be.[24] The goddess Skuld is connected with the word "scold" because She could speak deadly words that would curse a person with ill luck or death. The name Urd is connected with Urtha or Eartha, Mother Earth. It is also the name of the spring of wisdom that the Norns as a group tended; another name for this well was Mimir (Mother), although the name also belonged to an uncle of Odin.

The Norns lived at the Well of Urd near one of the roots of the World Tree Yggdrasil. As spinners of fate, time, and destiny, these deities ruled over both the gods and humans. The Norse gods could not give any judgement without meeting at the well of Urd. The fact that the water from this well turned everything white may tie these goddesses to the three phases of the Moon. They were also known as Die Schreiberinnen (the Writing Women), thus showing a firm connection with the attribute of fate.

Zorya

The English continued to know of the Norns by the name of the Weird Sisters.[25] The Anglo-Saxons called them by the name of Wyrd; in Old High German, Wurd.[26] In Macbeth, Shakespeare turned them into three Witches around a cauldron. However, eight centuries before this, the author of Beowulf wrote of the Goddess Wyrd who had the fate of every human written in Her book. Beowulf says that all decrees of Wyrd were final. These Wyrd Sisters are quite likely direct descendants of the Greek Moerae or Fates. During the Dark Ages these Three Sisters continued to be invited to the house of a newborn child; so they would be disposed to giving a good fortune, a feast was laid in their honor with three knives and goblets.

The Zorya of the Slavs were very similar to the Greek Moerae or Fates. They were called the Three Little Sisters: She of the Morning, She of Midnight, and She of Evening.[27] It was said that they kept the doomsday wolf chained to the pole star, and that if it breaks free, it will be the end of the world.

THE MUSES AND OTHER NINES

Nine is a number of the Crone aspect of the Goddess and of the Moon. It is a multiple of three, the number of the Goddess in general. Many of the goddesses who formed the groups of nine appear on the surface to have little to do with the Crone. Upon deeper study, one finds that these deities influenced inspiration, psychic abilities, prophecy, etc. These gifts are within the guidance of the Dark Mother.

The Muses, or Mousea, the daughters of Zeus and the Titaness Mnemosyne (Memory), were generally nine in number. As the Pierides, they ruled over the springs Kastalia, Aganippe, and Pimpla or Pimplea on the sides of Mount Helikon and Mount Parnassus; inspiration was said to be gained by drinking water from these springs. The Muses were especially worshipped on Mount Helikon where a sacred grove held many monuments to them. There, also, were the sacred fountains of Aganippe and Hippokrene. Special contests, called Museia, were associated with the ceremonies at these fountains.

Mnemosyne, or personified memory, was the daughter of Earth and sky. After nine days of continual lovemaking with Zeus, She gave birth to the nine Muses, or goddesses of art. Mnemosyne was called upon by ancient poets when reciting the sacred sagas, which were learned by rote.[1] Her nine daughters were born near Mount Olympus at Pieria,[2] a place they later made their dancing ground. The hunter Crotus raised them; when he died, he was placed in the sky as the bowman Sagittarius.

The Muses were connected with two gods of different types of divine inspiration: Apollo and Dionysus. Apollo, known as Musagetes when he traveled with the Muses, gave oracular and orderly inspiration, while Dionysus was known for his wild and excited nature.

Each of the Muses held the special power of a certain area of literature, art, song, memory, or science. Calliope ruled over epic poetry; Clio, history; Euterpe, lyric poetry; Melpomene, tragedy; Terpsichore, choral dance and song; Erato, love poetry; Polyhymnia, sacred poetry; Urania, astronomy; and Thalia, comedy.

The Muses and their areas of influence have evolved to meet modern requirements. Calliope, the leader, helps the writers and speakers of serious literature; Clio, the trumpet player, helps historians to record the past; Euterpe, the flute player, guides composers and those who play wind instruments; Melpomene still inspires those who write tragedies; Terpsichore, the guitarist, aids players of string instruments and dancers; Erato inspires writers of romantic prose and poetry; Polyhymnia assists actors and the creators of songs; Urania deals not only with astronomy but astrology; and Thalia looks after comedians.

The musical scale of seven tones was said to have originated with the Muses; they based it on the music of the seven planetary spheres. It was thought that anyone who could imitate this harmony of the lyre would be able to trace his or her way back to the celestial realm,[3] an allusion to tracing the labyrinth down through the seven chakras into the inner twisting path to the Divine Center.

A special complicated twelve-pointed interlacement of three triangles (nine sides) is a symbol related to the Muses and the zodiac signs.[4] In the city of Alexandria there was a great temple and school of the arts dedicated to the Muses; this was called the Museum. The word Muse is connected with the words music, amuse, and muse. The Persian-Arabic version of a fairy or nymph was called a Peri; this was a female spirit guide, often considered a kind of Muse. The Greeks said that Mount Helikon was the home of the Muses; the willow and willow wands for divination were sacred to them.

Hesiod wrote of three symbolic Muses: Melete (practicing), Mneme (remembering), and Aoide (singing). However, this trio was never particularly popular. Today, it is common to speak of the Muse in a singular sense.

The fair god Heimdall, a supporter of the goddess Freyja and watchman of the Bifrost bridge, was said to have had nine mothers. Heimdall was probably one of the original Vanir.[5] In some way, he was associated with the sea; the nine maidens who were said to be his collective mother may have been waves.

The sea goddess Ran had nine daughters by the sea god Aegir. Like their mother, these daughters were seen as both waves and mermaids. The poets called them "the claws of Ran." It was said that Ran drew drowned sailors down into Her realm as companions for Her daughters.

XII

THE VALKYRIES AND OTHER MULTIPLES

This group of goddesses is very complex, since groups do not always fall into the categories of multiples of three. It is possible that over the centuries their numbers have been altered to fit a patriarchal scheme.

The Valkyries were the warrioress attendants of the Norse god Odin. They directed the course of battles according to the wishes of the Allfather, choosing the most valiant warriors for Valhalla. They formed a link between Odin and the slain, the living and the dead. But certain females were also said to become Valkyries, giving rise to the possibility that these women may have been warrioress-priestesses dedicated to the god Odin.

In Old English the Valkyries were called Waelceasig, Waelcyrge or, as on an inscription found at Hadrian's Wall, the Alaisiagae; the equivalent in Icelandic was Valkyrja. Descriptions in Norse poems and prose picture them as helmeted goddesses with spears crowned with flames and mounted on flying horses whose manes dropped dew or hail.

The Norse-Germanic Valkyries were often spoken of as being three (rare), twelve, thirteen,[1] or more in number. The skalds called them battle-maids and death angels; the title Valkyrie means "chooser of the slain." In many ways the Valkyries are similar to the Greek Erinyes, although they did not exhibit the fierce defense of mothers and the blood line. When the Valkyries were associated with death, they often wore raven feathers, perhaps cloaks of such black feathers, onto the bat-tlefield to retrieve dead warriors.[2] The blood of these warriors was called "raven's drink."[3] Because they decided the karmic fate of warriors, the Valkyries were also similar to the Norns and Fates.

As shape-shifters they could change into swans, hawks, or mares. Like the ancient horse-masked priestesses of Demeter, the Valkyries rode horses and/or became mares; their earthly priestess-representatives likely wore the same type of horse-masks as their Grecian counterparts. In Swe-den, the volva (priestess) was said to be able to turn into a mare and carry a man away to his death, much as the Valkyries did on the battlefield. The Swedish title volva is related to other funerary words, such as Vala, Vila, and Wila.

In some myths, the Valkyries emerged as swan-maidens. These swan-maidens were able to put on or take off their swan skins at will. They possessed the ability to fly and were known for their ability to fore-tell the future. In this guise, the Valkyries were said to visit the Earth between battles and visit lonely lakes and forest ponds. If their plumage was captured by a human, these maidens were in the person's power until they could regain their disguise; in the myths, these captors were all men.

These warrior women were associated with horses, wolves, and ravens in particular. The raven and the wolf were regarded as creatures of Odin. The connection between the raven and the death-maiden Valkyries was not a new concept to the Norse. One of the earliest Old Norse poems, Hrafnsmal, is a dialogue between a raven and a Valkyrie.

Those initiated into the Orphic tradition were said to have a raven perched on their shoulder when they entered the temple for the metaphorical death and rebirth ceremony.[4] In the Mithraic tradition, when the initiate received the first degree of enlightenment he was given the title of Raven; this signified ascent to the realm of the Moon goddess who cared for the dead.[5]

The Valkyries were capable of binding or loosening fetters, chang-ing the course of battle, and answering to spells to accomplish these tasks. In both Havamal and Ynglinga Saga these traits are mentioned, although the fetters appear to be those of the mind rather than of the body. The war-fetter mentioned is not battle panic, but more a kind of paralysis of the mind, such as experienced in a nightmare.

The Valkyries appeared in dreams or visions as a warning of fighting and death. An example of such a dream vision is recorded in Njals Saga, a vision which was said to have occurred before the Battle of Clontarf in Dublin in 1014. This poem, known as the Darradarljod or Spear-Lay, describes a group of Valkyries as weaving on a loom made of men's entrails and weighted with severed heads; into a background of gray spears they were weaving a pattern of crimson blood. This depicts one aspect of the Valkyries: that it was they who worked out the fate of men in conflicts.

But other aspects of these women are described as well. Brynhild as Sigrdrifa (Victory-Giver) was a Valkyrie. She initiated Sigurd into runic wisdom. The Sigdrifumal, one of the poems of the Edda, is a treasure of rune magick. If the person of Sigrdrifa was in actuality a symbolic representation of a priestess of Odin, then this teaching makes sense, as would the depiction of the Valkyries casting binding spells in battle. For the Allfather took direct action, even interfered at times, in the lives of humans, and the runes were closely connected with him through his self-sacrifice to obtain them.

Although the Valkyries collected half the slain warriors for Odin and were considered to be the god's attendants, they were said to be under the authority of both Odin and Freyja. Freyja was called the leader of the Valkyries and collected Her own half of the heroes. The Eddas say the Valkyries were equally at home serving drinks in Valhalla or riding fully armored into battle.

The Valkyries appear to have been personifications of wild primal energies, as expressed by their names: Hlokk (the Shrieking One), Goll (the Screamer), and Skogul (the Raging One). Crossley-Holland lists their names as Shaker, Mist, Axe Time, Raging, Warrior, Might, Shrieking, Host Fetter, Screaming, Spear Bearer, Shield Bearer, and Wrecker of Plans.[6]

The god Odin has been looked upon as primarily a deity for males, one who has little appeal for women. If the Valkyries were priestesses of Odin, as is hinted at in Norse literature, then new doors are opened for females who are drawn to the Norse pantheon or just to a more self-assertive life style. Women who have a fierceness of spirit and determination will find in the Valkyrie way a new opening for magickal and spiritual growth. Using the power of the Valkyries to take charge of your life, stand up for yourself, and develop a more rounded, power-charged personality is a positive step for any person.

The Rhinemaidens of the Germanic myth of the Nibelungenlied were depicted as three in Wagner's Ring Cycle, but in other tales they were seen as being a greater number. They guarded the mystic gold and the magickal ring at the bottom of the River Rhine, a metaphor of the spiritual gold hidden within the wisdom and depths of the Goddess. Walker[7] says that the Nibelungs were spirits of the dead, the magickal ring was the karmic wheel, and the Rhinemaidens the keepers of the dead. Like the Greek Sirens, to hear the songs of the Rhinemaidens was to be called to physical death.

The Greeks tell of the 50 daughters, the Danaids, of Danaus who left Egypt for Thebes (some say Ireland). Aegyptus and his 50 sons chased Danaus and his 50 daughters back to their homeland of Argolis. Finally, the sons and daughters were married in a reconciliation. The story goes that 49 of the Danaids murdered their husbands on the wedding night.[8] Only the Danaid Hypermnestra did not participate. She and Lynceus started the royal house of Argos; the tribal name Danai was given to the Argives. It is possible that the Celtic-Irish goddess Danu, who gave Her name to the Tuatha de Danaan, may be connected to the Greek Danaids in some manner.

The sea god Oceanus had as many as 3,000 daughters who were known as the Oceanids. The myths of these females suggest that they had the ability to train dolphins and seals; it was said to be their task to supervise all waters and waterlife. Styx was the Oceanid mother of the goddess Nike, but all others were the offspring of the sea queen Tethys and the sea god Oceanus.

Probably the most important group of sea-goddesses were the 50 Nereids (wet ones), or Dorides as they were sometimes called. These were the daughters of Nereus and the Nymph Doris. Nereus, an ancient sea god, was the son of Pontos and Gaea; some sources say that the Nereids were the offspring of Pontos and Gaea rather than Nereus. The most famous of the Nereids were Amphitrite, Thetis, Panope, and Galatea. The Nereids were said to be quite beautiful and have oracular powers; having human-like forms, they cavorted naked through the ocean waves, often riding sea monsters. They could both predict and avert shipwrecks.

The Nereids Galene and Glauke produced the shimmering light on the gentle sea; Thoe and Halie the movement of the waves; Nesaie and Aktaee the rush of water on island shores; Pasithea, Erato, and Euneike the rising tide; Pherusa and Dynamene the swell of huge breakers; and Amphitrite led them all. The Water Nymphs are related to the Nereids, and both groups were often seen as mermaids.

Seven Sisters

Kali, the Dark Mother of India, is said to have ten facets or trans-formations; these are sometimes called the Mahavidyas. The Tantrists consider meditation of these facets an essential part of their spiritual growth. One of the facets most often pictured is Chinnamasta. In this aspect She is draped with snakes and holds Her severed head in Her left hand, while three fountains of blood spout from Her neck. These three streams of blood represent the gunas of Hindu belief, the symbolic depic-tions of the Triple Goddess.

The Seven Sisters of Roman-Greek mythology were called the Pleiades. Born in wild Arcadia, they were the daughters of the giant Atlas; they were the nymph companions of the goddess Artemis-Diana.[9] The giant Orion decided he wanted all seven of the daughters and gave chase. In answer to their prayers, Jupiter made them into a constellation; he also placed Orion and his dog Sirius in the heavens. This story of the Seven Sisters and Orion is known in many cultures around the world. Only six of the stars are visible; Electra, the seventh, hid to avoid seeing the destruction of Troy, founded by Her son Dardanus. Later Electra was changed into a comet, ranging the heavens in Her grief. The names of the Pleiades are given as Alcyone, Calaeno, Electra, Maia, Merope, Asterope, and Taygete.

PART VI
IMPORTANCE OF THE SACRED THREE TODAY

XIII

THE EVER-PRESENT
GODDESS

The single biggest loss to humankind is the loss of balanced individual spiritual direction. A great many people are not free, physically, mentally, or emotionally, to choose the spiritual path that best suits their needs. In some cases, they are prohibited from doing this by national laws and/or extreme peer pressure. Censorship often cuts off any opportunity for a person to investigate other spiritual ideas. The problem with censorship is that once it is given a foot in the door, so to speak, every spiritual idea can eventually fall under its axe. The greatest danger of denying anyone individual freedom within the laws of the land is that eventually those who foster the loss will suffer it along with the ones they persecuted.

Humankind has one major personality flaw that seems to be world-wide: people are always seeking for answers, especially to spiritual questions, outside themselves. They are always looking for an undefined something (which in reality is spiritual satisfaction) in other humans, organizations, work, frenetic play, drugs, and alcohol. A great many of us, at least in the beginning stages, are afraid of stillness and silence, the great Void of the Goddess that can only be reached through the dark labyrinth of the subconscious and collective unconscious minds. But as the Charge of the Wiccan says: "If you do not find Me within, you will never find Me without. For I was there in the beginning, and I will gather you to My breast at the end of all things."

You must train yourself to do listening as well as participating meditations. Both types of meditation have a place in the spiritual growth of an individual. Participating meditation is the most immediately rewarding; in fact, it can be fun and informative.[1] It brings physical results by relieving stress, mental results by calming and drawing the mind's attention away from irritating thoughts, and spiritual results by presenting other options to problems.

Listening meditation is more difficult. The most one can do with this type of meditation is visualize (or try to) the Goddess, mentally reaching for Her and listening. Ordinarily, any messages tend to come at a later time through dreams, sudden enlightenment through people or reading, or through an awe-inspiring burst of understanding. This linkage of communication is vital to humans in order to fully understand the inner self, why one is here (again), what one is supposed to be doing, and for re-establishing clearer communication with the Great Mother.

The secret of this connection is that it is the thread that binds us to the Great Mother. It is up to each of us to find and revitalize it. The Goddess has provided the eternal link; we must be the ones to open the channel and listen to Her words of guidance and wisdom. This listening, and its benefits, is not solely a woman-thing. Men also need reconnection with the Goddess.

The Goddess is the Divine Center of all. With great patience She awaits the return of Her children, Her divine creations. Seeking within, striving to find the way through the inner labyrinth, is the only path back to Her. Each individual must make the journey alone, following Her voice through the maze until, standing in Her lightless Light, each of us sees him or herself reflected in Her mirror of truth and realizes that he or she has not ever been alone.

Because of this instinctive seeking, many people are beginning to learn new ways of relating to other humans. They prefer partners in relationships. Children are more than possessions to them. They genuinely feel that each human, regardless of race, sex, or religion, is important and holds a spark of divinity. These are the people who listen to their creative subconscious; they are the dreamers of the future, the innovators of new ideas, the heralds for peace.

These men and women are willing to do whatever it takes to restore balance to the world, knowing that the resulting new form of society will benefit everyone. Others still experience a fear that they cannot put into words. Perhaps this fear stems from the fact that on the subconscious and collective unconscious levels all humans are aware that they come from and return to the Goddess. Everyone passes upward from the abyss through the creative spiral to existence and descends again into the chaos of dissolution. Death and rebirth cannot be stopped.

The entire universe operates on receptive/active, positive/negative, male/female combinations. The Goddess operates as She has always done despite rejection of Her.

For centuries, women have been behind the scenes leaders into the future, particularly on social issues. Early explorers had their women companions who followed with a pack on the back and a child by the hand. The first doctors were priestesses and midwives. Women herbalists experimented on themselves before treating patients with a new plant medicine. Because of being in greater touch with their emotions and intuition,[2] women were the first artists, weavers, potters, agriculturalists, and writers. Their intuitive feelings, honed over the centuries from taking care of children and their men, are valuable assets. But men, too, can open their intuition and strengthen it with use until it becomes a natural part of life.

Breaking many of the long-established societal patterns will not mean chaos. The key word for the future will be equality. Equality in all areas of life for everyone, combined with common sense and spiritual freedom, is essential for reforming nations and the world into a better place to live, learn, and raise the next generation. Women and men must help and encourage each other. Only together can we move along the Mother's cycles into a brighter future.

Women do not look at the world in the same way that men do. Females tend to look at their society and surroundings in terms of raising children and cultivating artistic and spiritual opportunities. Their example has led many men to follow the same pathway of ideas.

A return to the Goddess would create an inner peace with life by teaching people to realize and work with cycles. One does not need to fear extinction, for all are reborn.

There is no escape from the Goddess and Her cyclical laws. The collective unconscious knows this to be true. We see it in all physical cycles of life. Intuitively, we feel it and are drawn to seek for a "mother."

The Goddess was the beginning of all things, and She will end all things in Her own good time. We cannot escape Her, nor should we want to. She is a part of us as is Her consort, the Lord of Nature. Each individual contains both male and female hormones, a very minor kind of androgyny. In this manner, we are tiny replicas of the Goddess who, as Creatress, was androgynous in Her first creative form. This also makes each one of us part of each other.

By acknowledging the Goddess and bringing back equality for all, we stand to gain some very vital things: contentment with ourselves, each other, and life; the opportunity for spiritual advancement however we individually decide to go; acceptance and respect for the stages of life experienced by each human; and the knowledge to prepare for death and rebirth. These are the treasures hinted at in the myths. These are the things we seek when we take our journey into the labyrinth.

By continuing to refuse to acknowledge the Goddess, we are traveling blindfolded. Suspicion and distrust of another human because of his or her lifestyle, sex, religion, intelligence, skin color, or political preference is defeating to spiritual growth. We allow these types of prejudices to continue by denouncing the Goddess.

What should we expect by acknowledging the Goddess? A balance between Goddess and God is essential. The Great Mother was never without Her consort after the first creation. "As above, so below" is more than a high-sounding statement. The swirling of the universe is repeated in the atom and the DNA molecule. The balance between Goddess and God, female and male, should be repeated in human life. A respect for the Goddess in all Her creations and forms will be reflected in how we treat each other and this Earth. By acknowledging the Goddess, taking good care of our world, each other, and all other creatures will become as natural as breathing. The struggles between nations will be worked out at conference tables instead of battle fields. The arts and sciences will flourish, enriching and healing the world. Personal freedom to seek individual spiritual paths will create better balanced, happier people. The benefits are endless.

Whether you think of the Goddess as a deity, a supernatural being, an archetypal concept, or a state of mind does not matter. The myths are symbolic stories of spiritual journeys and abstract conceptions of the universe. They say that the Goddess, or Divine Creative Force, has set into motion certain immovable laws. Even if the myths are only symbolic stories, the human race knows enough history to realize they hold truths. Universal laws, however you perceive them, cannot be broken or circumvented without paying a penalty. We must learn to work with Her cycles of life for our own self-preservation as a species. And as trial and error has taught us, it is easier and more satisfying to work with the forces of Nature than against them.

Recognizing the ever-present Goddess benefits everyone: physically, mentally, emotionally, and spiritually. It takes away nothing. It creates a healthier, happier atmosphere in which to live. It is up to us. As the Wiccan Rede says: "If you do not find Me within, you will never find Me without." Acknowledging the Goddess must be an internal, intensely personal, individual experience, which will ripple outward to affect and revitalize this world and humankind. The only changes we can definitely make and control are within ourselves, one individual at a time. It is time to make a start.

PART VII

APPENDIX

XIV

MEDITATIONS

For all types of meditations, it is important that you have a comfortable chair and a place where you are unlikely to be disturbed. Put a "Do not disturb" sign on your door to discourage visitors, and silence the telephone. Soft, soothing music played during your meditation helps mask minor background noises that might distract you.

If you have very active pets who are not used to your sitting quietly for a time, you might consider shutting them out of the room in which you will be meditating. If possible, explain to family members and friends that this is your time for silence and solitude; if this is not possible, choose a time when you are least likely to be disturbed.

Some people like to burn incense while meditating. If you choose to do this—and it is often an added emotional help—do not place the incense too close or you might find yourself choking on the smoke. Some people find themselves very cold when emerging from a meditation. If you find this to be true for you, keep a sweater or blanket nearby.

Unless you are very experienced in yoga, do not attempt to sit cross-legged or in a lotus position. There is actually little to be gained from these positions, except leg cramps and numbness, unless you are deep into Eastern philosophies.

For the best positive results from a meditation, do not use alcohol or drugs. This is an excellent rule for your life anyway, but some people new to meditation have the misconception that these additives will aid them in their spiritual journey. Actually, the opposite is true. Misinformation and negative spiritual experiences have come from meditations influenced by alcohol and drugs.

Whenever you receive advice during a meditation, be very sure you are not hearing just what you want to hear. If you receive advice in an extreme form, question it closely. True spiritual advice never tells you to do anything unethical or extreme in nature.

Remember, you can end a meditation at any time; you are never locked into the experience. You control whether you stay or leave meditation.

The beginning and ending of the following three meditations are exactly the same so that you are in familiar surroundings as you progress with your spiritual experiences with the Goddess. After you have gone through these meditations several times, you will probably find changes, small or large, occurring. That is natural. Your subconscious and collective unconscious minds are tailoring the experiences to fit your spiritual needs.

The Maiden, Mother, and Crone may change appearances from one meditation to the next. They can, and do, change coloring and racial features, for the Triple Goddess is part of all people, all races, and all cultures.

Since the Goddess can only be experienced and found on an individual basis, these meditations are vital to the spiritual growth of all humans. The wonder and beauty is that they will never be quite the same twice. As we open more and more to each aspect of the Triple Goddess, the meditations expand accordingly. Even within a group meditation, individual experiences will rarely be identical. Expect wonderful things when you go on the inner journey to meet the Goddess. You will never be disappointed.

MAIDEN MEDITATION

Sit in a comfortable position with your feet flat on the floor and your hands in your lap. Close your eyes and visualize a white light coming into position over the top of your head. See it coming down over you until you are completely surrounded by the light. Breathe it in with slow, even breaths. Feel your body relaxing, beginning with your toes and working up to your jaw and head muscles. It may take more time to relax the muscles of the shoulders, neck, and head than the rest of the body.

Now see yourself standing beside a well. The stone walls of the well are moss-covered and worn. Take all the problems in your life that are bothering you (that includes people) and drop them into the well. Then turn and walk away down a little path that leads through a grove of trees.

In a short time you come to a very high cliff wall at the end of the path. Set into the wall is an iron-bound oak door. The door is narrow and tall with a peak at the top. A huge brass ring hangs near one edge of the door. You pull on the ring, and the door slowly comes open.

Inside is a wide tunnel winding away into the darkness, its curved roof illuminated for a space by two torches which hang in iron holders on either side of the door. As you step inside and take down one of the torches, the door slowly closes behind you.

Although the tunnel ahead is dark, the light of the torch clearly illuminates your way. You are protected. You set off down the tunnel, thinking of the Maiden. The tunnel begins to gently curve, first one way, then the other. There are smaller side tunnels but you feel no desire to explore them. You realize that you have at last entered the true labyrinth.

In the distance you hear the wild barking of dogs. You remind yourself that you are completely protected and have nothing to fear. Ahead of you are faint reflections of light, the sound of voices and footsteps. You go on, holding your torch high.

The sound of barking comes closer. Around a bend of the labyrinth comes a group of white-clad men and women, torches in their hands. Leading them is a tall, muscular woman dressed in a short white robe. Her hair is tied back, and at Her shoulder hang a bow and quiver of arrows. Hunting boots are on Her shapely feet. On Her right wrist an owl perches, its large, dark eyes peering at you. A pack of lean hounds jump around you, licking your hands and barking.

The Maiden stops before you. You gaze into Her eyes, taking in their color and the color of Her hair, Her skin. She beckons to you, then turns and leads Her followers back down the tunnel, deeper still into the labyrinth. One of the companions links arms with you and urges you forward. Together you follow the Maiden.

Soon the twisting tunnel widens into a circular room. In the center a spring bubbles up in a fountain set inside a wide, shallow bowl in the floor. A series of benches are placed along the curving walls. You and the group of companions all set your torches in holders in the walls. As you do this, you notice that the smooth, white walls are covered with bright murals and elaborate carvings.

You walk slowly around the circular room, looking at the murals of forests and animals, dancing people, and ritual scenes. The scenes and designs seem to touch something deep within you, as if you should understand a deeper mystical meaning behind them.

Soon one of the companions touches your arm and smiles. The companion points toward the Maiden who stands beside the central bowl of water. When you stand before Her, the Maiden smiles gently and asks if you have questions. The two of you talk for a time. She tells you that some of the answers will come later in dreams and in other ways.

Finally, She points to the spring and asks if you are prepared for initiation. If so, you slide quickly out of your clothes and step into the shallow basin. The Maiden picks up a pitcher and dips up the water. Slowly She pours pitcher after pitcher of the sparkling water over you as She and Her companions sing and chant. When She is finished, She blesses you with a kiss on the forehead. You feel your third eye begin to pulse and become active.

After you are again dressed, the companions and the Maiden lead you quickly back up the twisting tunnel. The journey back is much shorter than the journey inward. As you approach the door, the group dashes back down the tunnel laughing and calling farewells. You replace your torch in its holder, push against the door, and find yourself outside.

You take three deep, slow breaths and find yourself again in your chair in your present life surroundings. Sit quietly for a few moments to absorb what you experienced. If you like, make notes of your journey.

Be aware for the next few weeks, for messages and answers to questions may come from very unlikely places and people. Look at everything logically, though. Never take extreme answers at face value. Spirit never demands extreme or unethical action.

MOTHER MEDITATION

Sit in a comfortable position with your feet flat on the floor and your hands in your lap. Close your eyes and visualize a white light coming into position over the top of your head. See it coming down over you until you are completely surrounded by the light. Breathe it in with slow, even breaths. Feel your body relaxing, beginning with your toes and working up to your jaw and head muscles. It may take more time to relax the muscles of the shoulders, neck, and head than the rest of the body.

Now see yourself standing beside a well. The stone walls of the well are moss-covered and worn. Take all the problems in your life that are bothering you (that includes people) and drop them into the well. Then turn and walk away down a little path that leads through a grove of trees.

In a short time you come to a very high cliff wall at the end of the path. Set into the wall is an iron-bound oak door. The door is narrow and tall with a peak at the top. A huge brass ring hangs on one side of the door. You pull on the ring, and the door slowly comes open.

Inside is a deep tunnel, its curved roof illuminated for a space by two torches which hang in iron holders on either side of the door. As you step inside and take down one of the torches, the door slowly closes behind you.

The light of your torch illuminates the path before you, although the tunnel ahead is dark. You remember that you are protected; nothing can harm you. You set off down the tunnel which begins to gently curve, first one way, then the other. The small side tunnels do not interest you. Your goal is the Maiden's fountain, somewhere ahead in the labyrinth.

Before long you hear the eager whine and short barks of the hounds. Turning a corner, you find yourself in the circular white room. Flaming torches hang in brackets along the brightly-colored murals. The fountain in its shallow bowl in the center of the room bubbles softly.

The Maiden rises from a bench at the far side of the room. She smiles and beckons to you, then turns quickly and leads the way into another dark tunnel, the hounds running ahead of Her. You follow, your torch casting a circle of light around you.

The tunnel begins an intricate series of twists and turns, with more and more side tunnels. It has become a true maze, a revealing pattern of the intricacies of your inner mind.

You begin to see the flicker of strange images out of the corner of your eye. These are the "ghosts" of your past, of both this life and other lives, events or people with whom you still have things to resolve. If you feel any threat coming from these apparitions, call to the Maiden and She will protect you.

If any of these "ghosts" presses close and demands your attention, and if you feel able to confront the past, stop and try to communicate. The Maiden will wait for you. If you are not able to understand the problem that remains between you and this past image, simply ask forgiveness and give your blessing. Later dreams or events may clarify this.

The Maiden leads you deeper still into the twisting labyrinth. Soon you hear the sounds of drums and tambourines and the clash of a sistrum up ahead. A light flashes. The Maiden turns a corner, and you find yourself in a huge red-walled chamber. The ceiling is far above you. Around the walls are ornate benches of crystal, and in the center is another fountain. This fountain is set in a waist-high bowl with steps leading up to it on three sides. Its water is a deep, rich red color.

Scarlet-clad men and women dance around the fountain. They weave a line of rhythm and music as they circle around you. When you turn to watch them, you see the Maiden disappear back into the tunnel. You turn again to the fountain and, for the first time, see a woman at the far end of the cavern. With smiles and music, the dancers whirl away toward the mysterious woman. You follow.

The Mother sits on a magnificent carnelian throne, Her long hair loose over Her shoulders. Her blood-red gown flows over Her full breasts and pregnant belly. Across Her lap sprawls a cat, its green eyes watching you. The Mother smiles and holds out Her hands in welcome. As you move toward the throne, the dancers give a loud shout and go to sit on the benches, talking quietly among themselves.

At the Mother's feet is a padded bench. You sit on its velvet softness and look up into Her loving eyes. She reaches down one ring-adorned hand and caresses your face, your hair. When She speaks, Her voice is soft and full of compassion. You listen intently as She talks to you. You are free to ask questions. The Mother may or may not answer them at this time, depending upon your being open and willing to listen.

After a time, the Mother touches your breast over your heart, then holds out Her hand to one of the dancers. They bring Her an elaborate chalice filled with water from the fountain. She holds it to your lips with a smile, and you drink. She explains the personal significance of this magickal drink, for its purpose changes as you change.

You find the Maiden once again at your side. As you stand to leave, the Mother holds out Her arms and hugs you. Then you turn and follow the Maiden back up the twisting tunnel. The journey back is much shorter than the journey inward.

As you approach the door, the Maiden smiles and says farewell. You replace your torch in its holder and push against the door. Once more you find yourself outside.

You take three deep, slow breaths and find yourself again in your chair in your present life surroundings. Sit quietly for a few moments to absorb what you experienced. If you like, make notes of your journey.

Be aware for the next few weeks, for messages and answers to questions may come from very unlikely places and people. Look at everything logically, though. Never take extreme answers at face value. Spirit never demands extreme or unethical action.

CRONE MEDITATION

Sit in a comfortable position with your feet flat on the floor and your hands in your lap. Close your eyes and visualize a white light coming into position over the top of your head. See it coming down over you until you are completely surrounded by the light. Breathe it in with slow, even breaths. Feel your body relaxing, beginning with your toes and working up to your jaw and head muscles. It may take more time to relax the muscles of the shoulders, neck, and head than the rest of the body.

Now see yourself standing beside a well. The stone walls of the well are moss-covered and worn. Take all the problems in your life that are bothering you (that includes people) and drop them into the well. Then turn and walk away down a little path that leads through a grove of trees.

In a short time you come to a very high cliff wall at the end of the path. Set into the wall is an iron-bound oak door. The door is narrow and tall with a peak at the top. A huge brass ring hangs on one side of the door. You pull on the ring, and the door slowly comes open.

Inside is a deep tunnel, its curved roof illuminated for a space by two torches which hang in iron holders on either side of the door. As you step inside and take down one of the torches, the door slowly closes behind you.

The light of your torch illuminates the path before you, although the tunnel ahead is dark. You remember that you are protected; nothing can harm you. You set off down the tunnel which begins to gently curve, first one way, then the other. The small side-tunnels do not interest you. Your goal is the Mother's chamber beyond the Maiden's fountain, somewhere ahead in the labyrinth.

Before long you turn a corner and find yourself in the torch-lit white-walled room with the Maiden's fountain bubbling in its shallow bowl in the center. The Maiden stands near the entrance to another dark tunnel, Her hounds gathered at Her feet. She beckons to you, then turns and leads the way into the tunnel, the hounds running before you. You follow, your torch casting a circle of light around you.

You recognize the intricate twists and turns, the increase of side-tunnels, as the way to the Mother's chamber. If you see any "ghosts" from your past lives here, you may stop and communicate with them. If, however, you feel any threat coming from these apparitions, call to the Maiden and She will protect you.

The Maiden leads you deeper still into the twisting labyrinth. Soon you find yourself in the lighted, red-walled chamber with its crystal benches. The central fountain sounds like tiny bells as it falls into its bowl. The Maiden goes straight to the carnelian throne, where the Mother waits. On the back of the throne perches a white owl, its dark eyes staring at you.

In a soft voice, the Mother tells you to follow the owl. She gestures to the wall behind the throne. As you step past Her, you see a narrow opening outlined in crystal and amethyst points. She smiles encouragingly as you move toward the black tunnel. The owl leaves its perch and flies ahead of you, its white plumage glowing in the darkness.

You squeeze through the narrow opening. The tunnel is so narrow you can reach to each side and touch the crystal-studded walls. Without warning, your torch goes out, and you stand in complete darkness. Then you see the delicate flicker of light across the crystal walls. You squeeze around a corner and find yourself in a black-walled cave. The walls and ceiling are cloaked in deep shadows. The only light comes from an ornate lamp set on the low stone wall around a central pool. Just beyond the pool is a huge cauldron. The owl perches on the cauldron rim and looks at you.

You walk to the pool and lay your extinguished torch on the rocky floor. Gazing down into the still black waters of the pool, you may see scenes in the water—scenes from the past, the present, or the future. Do not be discouraged if nothing is revealed during this visit. Sometimes it takes more than one journey to this pool before one can see backward and forward through time.

Beyond the cauldron, you see a movement, and a black-robed figure steps forward. A hood covers the head and shadows the face. Two long gray braids hang down across the breast. You stand silent for a few moments, gazing at this powerful figure. You feel no menace coming from the figure, only concern and deep love.

Then leathery hands are raised and the hood dropped back to reveal an older woman, the Crone, the Dark Mother. Although She is aged, She is very beautiful. Her eyes are filled with timeless wisdom. She holds out Her hands and you go to stand directly before Her, gazing into those wise eyes.

The Crone gestures for you to sit beside Her at the edge of the pool. She asks if you have any questions about karmic patterns in your life. You may ask Her about any present event or person and how they fit in from other lifetimes. You may also ask about the future and how it is tied to the past. Confirmation or revelation of past lives is also within the realm of the Dark Mother. The Crone will give you the information She knows you will use in a positive way. She may, at times, refuse to answer until a later time. You can hide nothing from the all-seeing, all-knowing Dark Mother.

When you have finished your conversation, the Crone asks if you are ready for a rebirth. This can bring drastic changes, so think carefully before you decide. If you answer yes, She takes your arm and leads you to the far side of the huge cauldron where there are steps leading up to it. You climb the steps and stand looking down into its black interior. An inky, bubbling liquid fills the cauldron. The Crone speaks encouraging words in Her soft voice as you stand there. Finally, you leap into the cauldron and fall down into its blackness.

The cauldron experience is intensely personal. There is no single experience, therefore no way to describe it. You will, however, feel healing and strengthening taking place within your body, mind, and soul. You may even see or experience past lives. At last you feel the Crone's hands touch you, and you are lifted up again to stand at the top of the steps. Although you have been immersed in liquid, you are completely dry. The Dark Mother helps you down the steps and guides you to a black marble bench at the shadowed back of the cave. Both of you sit there while the Crone continues to instruct you and answer questions.

The Dark Mother takes a silver chalice from the floor near Her feet and holds it while you drink. The liquid is such a dark purple that it is almost black. It fills you with warmth, with hope, with renewal. The Crone gently touches the center of your forehead, your heart, and your belly. Where She has touched, there is a deep, intense feeling of warmth and energy. She presses into your hand a special symbol. This symbol may be entirely spiritual or may actually come to you in the physical at a later date.

The Dark Mother leans forward and kisses your cheek. Instantly, you are whirled away in a vortex of bright lights and melodic sounds. When the whirling stops, you find yourself once again at the exit door of the labyrinth. You push against it and go outside.

You take three deep, slow breaths and find yourself again in your chair in your present life surroundings. Sit quietly for a few moments to absorb what you experienced. If you like, make notes of your journey.

Be aware for the next few weeks, for messages and answers to questions may come from very unlikely places and people. Look at everything logically, though. Never take extreme answers at face value. Spirit never demands extreme or unethical action.

XV

RITUALS

Rituals can be as elaborate or as simple as you wish. There are certain actions which appear to be almost universal; these you can tailor to your spiritual beliefs. These actions provide protection against negative influences while you are working your ritual and also help to contain the power you are raising until you are finished with your work.

Incense has been used during rituals since ancient times. It does not matter whether you use incense sticks or cones, the kind that is burned on charcoal, or smudge sticks. Usually, the incense is presented to the Four Quarters at the beginning of the ritual as a purification of the area and you.

If you use Ceremonial Magick, cast your circle according to your particular practices. If Wiccan, you also cast the circle according to your usual procedure. Native Americans can smudge the area that they plan to use.

The following instructions are for greeting the Four Quarters. I have given simple examples using the Archangels, Elementals, and Native American animal helpers. These Quarters are greeted at the beginning of the ritual and dismissed at the end before you leave the sacred area.

Any area where you are working a ritual is sacred for the time you are there. You make it so by the purification of the area, your ritual and meditation, and your praise to the Goddess.

THE FOUR QUARTERS

ARCHANGELS

Greetings

Go to the East. Raise your power hand as you present the incense.

> Greetings, O Raphael, Prince of Brightness. Bring to me harmony, balance, and success in my endeavors.

Go to the South. Raise your power hand as you present the incense.

> Greetings, O Michael, Prince of Wisdom. Bring to me protection, knowledge, and the skill to see the truth in my endeavors.

Go to the West. Raise your power hand as you present the incense.

> Greetings, O Gabriel, Prince of Change. Bring to me visions, true magick, and prophecy in my endeavors.

Go to the North. Raise your power hand as you present the incense.

> Greetings, O Auriel,[1] Prince of Divine Light. Bring to me insight, endurance, and spiritual teaching in my endeavors.

Dismissal

Go to the East. Raise your power hand.

> Farewell, O Raphael. My thanks for your aid and protection.

Go to the South. Raise your power hand.

> Farewell, O Michael. My thanks for your aid and protection.

Go to the West. Raise your power hand.

> Farewell, O Gabriel. My thanks for your aid and protection.

Go to the North. Raise your power hand.

> Farewell, O Auriel. My thanks for your aid and protection.

ELEMENTALS

Greetings

Go to the East. Raise your power hand as you present the incense.

Greetings, Lords and Ladies of the East, you rulers of Air. I ask your aid during this ritual.

Go to the South. Raise your power hand as you present the incense.

Greetings, Lords and Ladies of the South, you rulers of Fire. I ask your aid during this ritual.

Go to the West. Raise your power hand as you present the incense.

Greetings, Lords and Ladies of the West, you rulers of Water. I ask your aid during this ritual.

Go to the North. Raise your power hand as you present the incense.

Greetings, Lords and Ladies of the North, you rulers of Earth. I ask your aid during this ritual.

Dismissal

Go to the East. Raise your power hand.

Farewell, Lords and Ladies of the East. Thanks for your help and protection.

Go to the South. Raise your power hand.

Farewell, Lords and Ladies of the South. Thanks for your help and protection.

Go to the West. Raise your power hand.

Farewell, Lords and Ladies of the West. Thanks for your help and protection.

Go to the North. Raise your power hand.

Farewell, Lords and Ladies of the North. Thanks for your help and protection.

POWER ANIMALS[2]

Greeting

Go to the East. Here are the big predators, such as lions, tigers, wolves, panthers, and boars. Wave the smudge stick.

Greetings, O mighty Power Animals of the East. Be with me and guard me now.

Go to the South. Here are such animals as bears, horses, apes, and elephants. Wave the smudge stick.

> *Greetings, O mighty Power Animals of the South. Be with me and guard me now.*

Go to the West. Here are water animals, such as fish, whales, squid, dolphins, otters, and seals. Wave the smudge stick.

> *Greetings, O mighty Power Animals of the West. Be with me and guard me now.*

Go to the North. Here are birds, such as eagles, crows, ravens, hawks, and falcons. Wave the smudge stick.

> *Greetings, O mighty Power Animals of the North. Be with me and guard me now.*

Wave the smudge stick skyward, then toward the Earth.

> *Greetings, O Father Sky and Mother Earth. Be with me and guide me during this ritual.*

Dismissal

Go to the East. Either raise your power hand or beat softly on a drum.

> *Farewell, O mighty Power Animals of the East. My thanks for your help and protection.*

Go to the South. Either raise your power hand or beat softly on a drum.

> *Farewell, O mighty Power Animals of the South. My thanks for your help and protection.*

Go to the West. Either raise your power hand or beat softly on a drum.

> *Farewell, O mighty Power Animals of the West. My thanks for your help and protection.*

Go to the North. Either raise your power hand or beat softly on a drum.

> *Farewell, O mighty Power Animals of the North. My thanks for your help and protection.*

Raise your hands to the sky, then touch the floor or Earth.

> *Farewell, Father Sky and Mother Earth. My thanks for your help and protection. Guide me always onto the right path.*

MAIDEN RITUAL

Try to time this ritual with the First Quarter or Waxing Moon for the best results. Read the section on the Maiden and magick so you will understand what aid She can give. You may add the name of any Maiden Goddess, if you wish. You will need a white candle, incense, a chalice or cup of juice,[3] a small dish of common salt, pencil and paper, and a metal bowl if you plan to burn the paper. You will want a small table or stand for an altar with a chair or pillows for sitting. Decorations of deer, forest animals, and white stones are in the area, if possible.

Light the incense and greet the Four Quarters. Hold your hand over the dish of salt and ask the blessings of the Goddess. Lightly sprinkle salt in a circle around your area; a few grains of salt along the edges work just fine. Seat yourself on the chair or pillows before the table. Light the white candle. Write out on the paper the goals you wish to accomplish.

> *Beautiful Maiden of the forests, Huntress of the soul, I call upon You to be here with me now. I need Your guidance as I strive for spiritual knowledge and growth. Help me also with (state your magickal purpose). I wish with all my heart to accomplish these desires in a positive way. If these are not to my good, reveal to me the direction to take, and the goals to which I should aspire. I await Your guidance and direction.*

Sit quietly for a few moments concentrating upon your wishes. You can do the Maiden Meditation now if you wish. You may also lay out the Tarot cards, cast the runes, or do another form of divination. Remember, you may not receive answers until a later time. Be patient. When you are finished with the silent meditation, fold the paper, light it from the candle, and drop it into the metal bowl to burn. If you do not want to burn it, tear it into small pieces that you dispose of later.

> *I give my desires and dreams into Your keeping. By Air, I create the seed. By Fire, I warm it. By Water, I nourish it. By Earth, I cause it to grow. From Spirit, I draw the power to make all things possible. Join me in celebration of the power of the Goddess.*

Hold up the chalice, then drink from it.

> *Thank you, lovely Maiden.*

Dismiss the Quarters. Extinguish the candle. Dispose of the torn paper or the ashes.

MOTHER RITUAL

Try to time this ritual with the Full Moon for the best results. Read the section on the Mother and magick so you will understand what aid She can give. You may add the name of any Mother Goddess, if you wish. You will need a red candle, incense, a chalice or cup of juice, a small dish of common salt, pencil and paper, and a metal bowl if you plan to burn the paper. You will want a small table or stand for an altar with a chair or pillows for sitting. Decorations of cats, doves, dolphins, and red stones are in the area, if possible.

Light the incense and greet the Four Quarters. Hold your hand over the dish of salt and ask the blessings of the Goddess. Lightly sprinkle salt in a circle around your area; a few grains of salt along the edges work just fine. Seat yourself on the chair or pillows before the table. Light the red candle. Write out on the paper the goals you wish to accomplish.

> Great Mother, ripe Creatress of all that exists, I call upon You to be here with me now. I need Your guidance as I strive for spiritual knowledge and growth. Help me also with (state your magickal purpose). I wish with all my heart to accomplish these desires in a positive way. If these are not to my good, reveal to me the direction to take, and the goals to which I should aspire. I await Your guidance and direction.

Sit quietly for a few moments concentrating upon your wishes. You can do the Mother Meditation now if you wish. You may also lay out the Tarot cards, cast the runes, or do another form of divination. Remember, you may not receive answers until a later time. Be patient. When you are finished with the silent meditation, fold the paper, light it from the candle, and drop it into the metal bowl to burn. If you do not want to burn it, tear it into small pieces that you dispose of later.

> I give my desires and dreams into Your keeping. By Air, I create the seed. By Fire, I warm it. By Water, I nourish it. By Earth, I cause it to grow. From Spirit, I draw the power to make all things possible. Join me in celebration of the power of the Goddess.

Hold up the chalice, then drink from it.

> Thank you, Great Mother.

Dismiss the Quarters. Extinguish the candle. Dispose of the torn paper or the ashes.

CRONE RITUAL

Try to time this ritual with the New Moon or dark of the Moon for the best results. Read the chapter on the Crone and magick so you will understand what aid She can give. You may add the name of any Crone Goddess, if you wish. You will need a black[4] candle, incense, a chalice or cup of juice, a small dish of common salt, pencil and paper, and a metal bowl if you plan to burn the paper. You will want a small table or stand for an altar with a chair or pillows for sitting. Decorations of black cats, owls, wolves, ravens, cauldrons, and black stones are in the area, if possible.

Light the incense and greet the Four Quarters. Hold your hand over the dish of salt and ask the blessings of the Goddess. Lightly sprinkle salt in a circle around your area; a few grains of salt along the edges work just fine. Seat yourself on the chair or pillows before the table. Light the black candle. Write out on the paper the goals you wish to accomplish.

> *Dark Mother, Guardian of the Akashic Records, Keeper of the Great Cauldron of Life, I call upon You to be here with me now. I need Your guidance as I strive for spiritual knowledge and growth. Help me also with (state your magickal purpose). I wish with all my heart to accomplish these desires in a positive way. If these are not to my good, reveal to me the direction to take, and the goals to which I should aspire. I await Your guidance and direction.*

Sit quietly for a few moments concentrating upon your wishes. You can do the Crone Meditation now if you wish. You may also lay out the Tarot cards, cast the runes, or do another form of divination. Remember, you may not receive answers until a later time. Be patient. When you are finished with the silent meditation, fold the paper, light it from the candle, and drop it into the metal bowl to burn. If you do not want to burn it, tear it into small pieces that you dispose of later.

> *I give my desires and dreams into Your keeping. By Air, I create the seed. By Fire, I warm it. By Water, I nourish it. By Earth, I cause it to grow. From Spirit, I draw the power to make all things possible. Join me in celebration of the power of the Goddess.*

Hold up the chalice, then drink from it.

> *Thank you, Dark Mother.*

Dismiss the Quarters. Extinguish the candle. Dispose of the torn paper or the ashes.

XVI

CLUES TO THE MYTHOLOGICAL MAP AND THE GODDESS WITHIN

Mythologies are vivid with images both strange and mundane. These images are all clues to the path leading through the maze of the mythological map, guiding the seeker deep into the subconscious and even deeper into the collective unconscious, that shared, common reservoir of knowledge belonging to all humans. By consciously understanding the meaning of these symbols, the seeker becomes more aware of them in mythologies, dreams, and meditations. This is one of the first steps toward finding the Divine Center. The ancient priestesses and priests constructed the myths out of spiritual, inward-guiding signs for just this reason.

Certain symbols reoccur, although the diverse cultures were unconnected. This points to the worldwide knowledge by spiritual leaders on how to contact the collective unconscious and hear the deities' voices which speak there.

As with all symbols, although the basic interpretation must remain the same, the meanings have to be brought forward into modern language and understanding. We should not try to re-create the old spiritual ways in entirety for they are not applicable to us now. The underlying spiritual ideas and paths are still of use; the methods of understanding and using them have changed.

When the word negative is used, it does not mean bad or evil. Negative is just another form of energy within the spiritual that balances its opposite, positive, and teaches in a different way. Female is called negative because that power tends to be more receptive than active.

Following is a list of symbols, by no means complete, which will help guide the seeker through the hidden spiritual meanings of myths, dreams, and meditations. The symbols will also mark the path through the labyrinth on the consciously-taken inward journey so that the seeker may reach the Divine Center, the doorway to the inner abiding place of the Goddess. The goddesses associated with these symbols have been listed in some places, but the connections listed are in no way complete.

Abyss: the land of the dead; one of the dwelling places of the Great Mother as both Mother and Crone. The neutral resting place of the creative primordial matter of chaos, or the state of unformed forms. The recycling center of the Great Goddess, where She reforms energy and matter that has outlived its usefulness in its previous forms. Also applies to canyon, void, or chasm.

Ambrosia: the feminine mysteries of the menstrual cycle; the re-creative power of menstrual blood. Called *soma* among the Hindus; red claret of the fairies, wise blood. Also see **potion.**

Androgyne, hermaphrodite: balance of opposites. The androgynous diamond shape is composed of the fused female and male triangles. Many of the creating goddesses were androgynous.

Ankh: the life symbol.

Apple: immortality;[1] earthly desires;[2] renewing; death and rebirth. Idunn, Hera.

Arms: means of activity. Four arms represent the union of male and female principles.

Arrows: divine intervention of both healing and killing power.

Baptism: confer divinity, bless. A ritual that represented re-birth; used long before the Christians. The priests of the Thracian goddess Cot-tyto (Crone) were called *baptes*.[3]

Bat: in China, good fortune and happiness; in Europe, a companion creature of Hel. The Christians made it a demonic creature; this is where the expression "a bat out of Hell" comes from. At one time it was believed that women's hair enticed demons, so they should cover the head; this is the origin of tales of bats getting caught in the hair. Actually, bats can avoid such hap-penings with their sonar.

Ankh

Bathing: purification.

Bear: unpredictable emotions. Sacred to Callisto and Artemis/Diana.

Bees: in the Indo-Aryan and Greek Orphic teachings these were the souls.[4] Every winged being was considered symbolic of the spiritual in one way or another. Called the Little Servants of the Goddess by early matriarchies; also the title of Aphrodite's high priestess on Mount Eryx. Demeter was sometimes called "the mother bee."

Blindness: inability or refusal to see what is happening in reality.

Blood: all liquids (even milk, honey, and wine) offered to the deities were symbolic of blood. Salted water used by the Wiccans has the same meaning; since many myths say that the Great Mother created all life from the seas, and blood has a salty taste, this is an apt metaphor. The words "blessing" and "blood" are related. Originally, altars were consecrated by their sprinkling with blood; now objects and people are sprinkled with salt water. Red is always considered the color of life. Red is the color of the Mother aspect of the Triple

Goddess, a sign of Her fruitfulness through menstruation and birth. The red dye henna was widely used by ancient worshippers of the Goddess; the staining of hands and feet was practiced by followers of Hecate, Anath, and many Hindu goddesses.

Box: with a lid, this is a female symbol (although a square is a male symbol) many times connected with the subconscious mind. The myth of Pandora's box was mutilated to become a coffer of terror and death. The subconscious mind can be a place of terror if the seeker journeying through it is unprepared.

Breasts: bare breasts often represented the priestesses who performed sexual initiations; the source of life-power and life-giving fluids from the Mother.

Bridge: this represents a link between heaven and Earth, or the subconscious and conscious minds. Bifrost, the bridge of Norse myth which spanned the heavens between Asgard and Midgard, is a good example.

Bridle: control over the physical body and the things that motivate a person to react through emotional responses.

Bull: at first this was a lunar symbol of the Great Mother, the horns being emblematic of the crescent Moon. Later, it became a symbol of the Sun gods, such as Attis and Mithras, both associated with Cybele.

Butterfly: the soul. The Greek word *psyche* means both soul and butterfly; in Ireland, Cornwall, Mexico, and Siberia, white butterflies are believed to be the spirits of the dead.

Castration: impotency in the use of energy; freedom from physical desires; failure.

Cat: stealth, independence, resourcefulness, healing. To the Egyptians[5] this was a Moon creature; cats were sacred to Isis, Bast, Artemis, Diana, and Freyja. During the Middle Ages, when the goddess Diana became known as the Queen of the Witches, the cat began to be associated with Witchcraft or Goddess worship. The belief that cats have nine lives may have come from Diana's association with the nine Muses.

Cauldron: the belly-vessel of rebirth; the first recycling center run by the Goddess. The Celts located this sacred cauldron deep under oceans or lakes, a metaphor of the amniotic fluid of birth and life's evolution from the seas.

Cave: another womb symbol.

Centaurs: healing energies which can get out of control and destroy if one does not properly control them. This image may have originated among the Greeks when they saw the horse-riding Amazons and other tribes of Central Asia. The centaurs were credited with shape-shifting, great magick, knowledge, hunting, medicine, music, and divination.[6]

Cat

Center: to move from the outer edges, the circumference, to the center is to move from the exterior to the interior, from diverse forms to one form, from created being to contemplation of creation, from time to no time. The center contains the treasure of knowledge that is of divine origin and can be reached only through spiritual seeking.

Chains: slavery to the physical and material. Sometimes a symbol that some actions and emotions must be controlled. A loss of freedom, often through karmic circumstances.

Chalice: same as the **cauldron.** The image of the Holy Grail was borrowed straight from the cauldron of the Goddess. In fact, the name Grail probably was lifted from the word "greal," the potion brewed by Cerridwen in Her cauldron in Wales.

Chaos: Plato and the Pythagoreans termed this the primordial matter of the world. Even Blavatsky said that chaos contains the seeds of universal creation. To the alchemists, the prime matter was the *proto-hyle* or *massa confusa*, from which anything could be created. Chaos has within itself all opposing forces, but they are in a state of dissolution, waiting within the void or abyss for the Great Mother to call them forth and mold them. It is a reasonable assumption to say that this term applies to the collective unconscious, which is full of creative but unformed energy.

Chariot: to Jung, the chariot represented the human body, the horse the life-force, and the driver the self. This is true also in Qabalistic writings. In myths the chariot is often driven by deities or fairies (Fates). The type of animal pulling it, its appearance and color, determines whether it has positive or negative qualities.

Child: symbol of the future and the deeply hidden treasure in the mystic center. Jung called this a protective, formative force coming from the subconscious. Dreams of a child portend a spiritual change coming, the beginning of a new cycle. Oftentimes in myths, the child teaches wisdom and solves riddles.

Circle: in later interpretations, the circle stood for the Sun and the Sun god. However, in the beginning it symbolized the vagina or birth-track opening of the Great Mother. Standing within the circle signified a return from multiples to unity, from time to timelessness, from the body-obsessed consciousness to the spiritual-centered subconscious. The Chinese yin-yang symbol of black and white dividing a circle represents a balance of male/female, positive/negative, energy/inertia, activity/passivity. The white spot in the black and the black spot in the white signify that there is always male in female and female in male.[7] Jung calls the circle the ultimate state of Oneness.

Circumference: if seen from within, it represents restriction or definition of an area; if seen from without, this symbolizes defense of the psychic, sensitive contents of the subconscious and soul. In myths and

Chariot

alchemy, dragons or serpents biting their tails are emblems of time and all cyclic systems.[8]

Clouds: possibility of fertility by divine forces or energies. Sometimes a temporary period of discomfort or distress. In myths from India, clouds and elephants are connected. In China, the clouds were female, the rain male. Clouds and halos are very similar.

Clover or trefoil: an emblem of the Triple Goddess. One obvious example of this was found among the Celts, to whom the shamrock[9] represented the three Mothers long before Patrick stole the idea to express the Christian trinity. Almost all trinity symbols date back to the time of the Goddess religions when they represented the Maiden, Mother, and Crone. In later Christianized Europe, people clung to the idea that three was holy and believed that to repeat anything three times was to do magick.[10]

Cobra: the kundalini force of the chakras. Two intertwined snakes, usually around a central staff, were also a sign of healing through the rising kundalini force.

Cobweb: associated with the spider, another emblem of the Goddess and the spinners, or Fates. It is the spiral shape of the creative matrix that leads inward to the center where matter is destroyed before being reformed. Scientists say that the universe is spiraling inward toward eventual destruction. Of course, Pagans know that the universe will continue spiraling through this destruction back into creation. Minerva and Athene were connected with spiders and spinning, as was the Native American Spider Woman.[11]

Color: there are many definitions of colors, probably as many as there are writers of spiritual ideas. The primary colors concerned with the Goddess, however, are white (Maiden), red (Mother), and black (Crone). These are discussed individually in the chapters on the specific aspects.

Column: the world axis, world tree, shamanic ladder, etc. One meaning is a connection between heaven and Earth, or gods and mortals, much as the bridge. When singular, the column came to be a phallic symbol, especially of fertility gods; megalithic stones and menhirs fall into this category. When in pairs, the column signified the balancing of opposing forces. Ancient symbols of the goddess Ceres were the column for love and the dolphin for the sea, or creation.

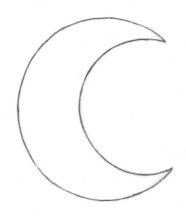

Crescent

Cone: may have been derived from the pyramid or a circle and triangle. A symbol of psychic Oneness. In ancient Byblos, it was a symbol of Astarte.

Copulation: planting seeds, as in magick, the physical, or mental ideas.

Cornucopia: in the story of the goat Amalthea feeding the infant Zeus, the cornucopia is a horn, a symbol of both maternal and phallic importance. It stands for strength and prosperity.

Cow: Earth and Moon. The life-giving and sustaining power of creation. A symbol of the Egyptian goddesses Hathor and Neith, and the female aspect of the Hindu god Brahma. The Norse goddess Audhumla was a cow; She licked the first being into existence.

Crane: from China to the Mediterranean the crane was an emblem of justice, longevity, and the purposeful soul.

Creation: in Egyptian hieroglyphics this was symbolized by several signs: a spiral for cosmic energy; a squared spiral for this energy working within matter; a square for matter finally organized. Bringing into being by combining positive and negative; making forms out of primordial matter of chaos.

Cremation: often connected with a sacrifice. The destruction of what is base and mundane in order for the superior or higher spiritual to come through.

Crescent: the Moon; the feminine principle; the world of changing forms which goes through a cycle to repeat itself again and again.

Crocodile: in Egypt this meant mindless fury and evil, and, strangely enough, knowledge.

Cromlech: a circle of monoliths enclosing a mound. Mircea Eliade defines this as fertility and health, citing certain folk customs which still remain. See **stone**. It is a symbol of the Great Mother, with the opening identical to the entrance of the birth canal.

Cross: this was used long before Christianity appropriated the symbol and changed its meaning. It appeared in many modified forms, such as the Egyptian ankh and the Aryan swastika, and is another form of the column or world tree. A symbol of the masculine principle of creation.

Crossroads: a Mother symbol; Jung called it a union of opposites. It was particularly sacred to the triform Hecate. The joining or mixing of positive/negative, male/female energies for creating anything; choices. Connected with certain forms of magick.[12]

Crow: because of its color, primordial darkness; maternal night of the abyss or void; creative power and spiritual strength found through the Crone aspect. To Native Americans, the crow was the great civilizer and creator of the visible world. There were similar meanings among the Celts, the Germanic tribes, and certain clans in Siberia. An emblem of the Celtic goddess Morrigan. Among many ancient cultures the crow was said to have mystic powers of foresight. The raven is similar.

Crown: different from hats, since sovereignty was originally ordained by the gods. It is a sign for light and spiritual enlightenment. Jung considered this the highest symbol of humankind conquering the rebellious and ego-centered self. The ancient Egyptian crown was topped with a rising cobra, symbol of the kundalini force guided by the gods through the ruler for the spiritual good of the nation.

Crystal: spirit and spiritual intellect. Also an emblem of the conjunction of opposites for, although crystal is obviously formed matter, its transparency leads one to half-believe it does not exist in matter.

Cube: the equivalent of the square; the material world of the four Elements; stability. A masculine symbol.

Cupbearer: messenger, sometimes from the higher deities.

Curl, loop, rope: binding and unbinding, especially in a magickal or spiritual sense. The spiritual umbilical cord that leads through the inner labyrinth to the Divine Center.

Curtain, veil: the ethereal door between the worlds of matter and spirit. Sometimes cloaks fall in this category. Parting or rending veils or divesting oneself of cloaks or bracelets symbolizes the penetration of a mystery. Images of the Crone aspect were often veiled as She was goddess of both death and the future. Sometimes there were seven veils representing the planets, as with Ishtar and Isis.

Cyclops: unpredictable, uncontrolled emotions which lead us into having tunnel vision. If the emotions are controlled, this vision becomes that of intuition, which can build great things. Sometimes the unpleasant lessons of life and their consequences.

Cypress: to the Greeks a tree sacred to the underworld deities. A symbol of death; returning to the abyss or void.

Dance: a sign of creating, becoming, the passage of time. The dance of Shiva is a good example as he dances space and time into evolution. But the first Dancer was the Goddess who created by movement over the waters of chaos without words. Movement that is repeated in a rhythmic manner is said to build up energy and make it easier to contact deities. See **procession.**

Darkness: the same as abyss and void.

Deafness: inability or refusal to hear what is happening in reality. The physical disability sometimes is a punishment.

Death: the end of an era, epoch, or cycle; often associated with sacrifice.

Decapitation: separation of the physical from the spiritual. The head was viewed as the holder of the spirit by some cultures, hence the preservation of heads among the Celts and others.

Deer, hind, doe: the guide for adventures of mystical value.

Deluge: the destruction of form followed by the re-emergence of new life. A tradition found in all parts of the world except Africa. Eliade relates it to the three days of the Moon's total darkness.

Desert: freedom from physical distractions so that spiritual revelations can take place. The Hebrews used this symbol to mean those having the only correct religion, as compared to the fertility religions of the agrarian communities.

Destruction: much the same as deluge.

Dew, rain: spiritual illumination; ideas sent by the Divine Source; sometimes forgiveness.

Dice: gambling with Fate; taking chances. The Charities.

Disk: emblem of the Sun and sometimes the heavens (as in China). A winged disk represents matter in a state of transformation.

Dismemberment, breaking into pieces: multiplicity out of unity; moving away from the center. The story of Siegmund's sword being broken into pieces is an example; his son, Siegfried, was the only one capable of reforging it into one piece again, although he never managed to do it.

Distaff: time and continuing creation; sometimes a sexual symbol. The Fates who spun, measured, and determined the length of life were connected with the distaff.

Dolphin: prudence, speed, active form-seeds within the sea-womb of creation. Themis.

Door: same as the opening of the cromlech; entrance to the path leading to the Mother.

Double: two of anything symbolizes balanced forces or opposite forces held in check.

Dove: the soul or spiritual being; a messenger from the gods. A symbol of Aphrodite, Astarte, and Venus; in Asia Minor the dove represented many aspects of the Great Goddess. Herodotus wrote that seven women called Doves founded the oracles of Dodona and Thebes. The dolphin and the dove are connected with the Maiden aspect of the Goddess.

Dragon: a universal symbolic figure found in most cultures around the world; has several, sometimes contradictory meanings. Its colors often correspond to the planets and the signs of the Zodiac. A wingless dragon is the self or ego as an oftentimes unpredictable force; winged, the ability to rise above and conquer obstacles.

Dreams: prophecy, guidance.

Drum: the world and the element of Earth. In shamanic traditions, the shaman used the drum beat to go into her/his subconscious mind where she/he can find answers to problems.

Duplication: multiplication of power; positive/negative principles. See **double.**

Dwarf: guardian of the threshold between the conscious and subconscious minds. Can be either positive or negative, depending upon the emotional and spiritual state of the person trying to cross the threshold.

Eagle: originally, the ability to reach spiritual heights. Later, from the Far East to Northern Europe, associated with the gods of Sun, power, and war.

Ear of corn: disintegration of life followed by rebirth. Associated with the Earth Mother, such as Ceres and Demeter.

Earthquake: sudden changes.

Egg: immortality; potential for renewing of life.

Elephant: strength and power of the libido; wisdom; eternity. Associated with clouds in India.

Enchantment: transformation, sometimes into a lower state, as with princes being turned into frogs. Other times the enchantment is of a higher nature, as with the tale of Cinderella who becomes, for a time, a well-dressed princess.

Eye: intelligence, spiritual light; judgement by the Goddess. Often associated with the Sun and/or Moon, especially in ancient Egypt. Archaeology has uncovered many little Eye Goddesses from Mediterranean and European areas, so it would appear that the patriarchal gods took this symbol from the earlier matriarchal goddesses.

Face: the self; emotions displayed on the face can reveal the true inner self of a person.

Fairies, feys: supernormal and psychic power; fate. In surviving folk tales, often the fairies, or feys, appear to be remnants of the Fate goddesses and appear in threes. Many times they were called fairy godmothers.[13] The ancient matriarchs, which were later turned into gods or supernatural beings, such as the Norse *disir*, the Celtic feys, and the Greek Titans.

Fan: phases of the Moon; femininity, intuition, change.

Farmer: a catalyst for regeneration and growth.

Father: the conscious mind; the male principle of creation.

Feather, plume: truth (as with the Egyptian goddess Maat and Her feathers on the scale when the soul was weighed at death), faith, contemplation. Symbol of the Element of Air and reincarnating souls. In Egypt, they believed each person had seven souls called the *ba*. Juno and many other goddesses had feathers ceremonially used in their temples; on the Isle of Man the Goddess's sacred bird was the wren.

Feces, manure: wealth, fertility, gold, prosperity.

Fields: unlimited potential. Earth gods and goddesses were associated with fields and their crops.

Fight: conflict between opposites.

Fire: to the Chinese, symbol of the Sun and the Element of Fire. To the Egyptians, the Sun and spiritual strength. To those in India, destruction and regeneration. In Africa and other tropical regions, danger and destruction. The life spark of the Goddess that burns deep within each person. Hestia, Vesta, Brigit, Anu.

Fish: the subconscious mind and divination. Many Mediterranean and Asian cultures connected fish with the Great Mother and the sea, thereby making it a symbol of sexuality and fertility. Fish, womb, and dolphin had similar meanings.

Flag, banner: victory, self-assertion. Sometimes a statement, positive or negative, of intentions.

Flight: the soul escaping the trap of addiction to physical sensations; an attempt to raise oneself above the mundane.

Flogging: purification. In some cultures, used to drive out demons.

Flower: separate meanings for different kinds, but generally connected with spring and rebirth or renewal.

Flute: the shape is masculine and phallic, but the notes feminine and intuitive.[14]

Flute

Fly: astral travel. Capes, especially feathered ones, are often metaphors for astral travel.

Foam: semen, as in the ocean foam that arose when Uranus's genitals were dropped into the sea.

Foot: humankind's connection with the Earth; foundation in the physical. Among the Greeks, Hindus, and Norse, often signified the departure of the soul. Henna-dyed feet were a sign of and dedication to the Goddess. Many ancient peoples, including the Egyptians and Babylonians, believed that to absorb sacred power from the Goddess one had to stand in bare feet in Her temples and sacred places. Roman priestesses performed rites with loose hair and bare feet for this reason.[15]

Ford: dividing line between two planes of existence. Anything rising out of the waters of a ford symbolizes ideas rising out of the subconscious; the interpretation depends upon the creature that arises.

Forest: the events of life; the mental and emotional qualities of the mind. Further interpretation depends upon whether the forest is light and airy or dark and foreboding. Originally connected with the female principle and the Maiden aspect; the dark, mysterious subconscious mind. Later it came to be the abode and under the control of the Goddess's consort, the Lord of the Forest.

Fountain: blessings, wisdom, purification, renewal, comfort arising from the center, or the Mother.

Friday: a day sacred to the Goddess, especially Freyja. Considered a lucky day if one believed in the old gods.

Frog: fecundity coming from the transition between two worlds; a lunar animal. In Egypt, Hekat the frog goddess was connected with birth.

Fruit: similar to the egg.

Garden: the conscious mind and its orderly methods, as opposed to the forest of emotions. The Mother's regenerating womb.

Gates: the chakras.

Ghosts: remaining spiritual energy of a person; memories of a person's past.

Giant: rebellion, dissatisfaction; the primitive emotions that humanity must keep under control.

Globe, sphere: wholeness; the world-soul.

Goblet: same as chalice and cauldron.

Gold: superiority; an advanced state. Later corresponded to the Great God as silver corresponds to the Great Mother.

Golden fleece: supreme strength of the spirit; quest of the impossible.

Goose: creativeness and spiritual guidance in destiny. The Great Mother who gave birth to the world; associated with several goddesses. The goose was so sacred to the Celts that they would not eat it.[16]

Goblet

Gorgon: the head of Medusa that petrified with a glance; it was hung on Athene's shield. The destructive power of kundalini (snake hair) when not properly raised.

Grain, wheat, corn: life and the sustaining of life. The growing grain symbolizes life after it has been planted.

Grapes: fertility and sacrifice.

Groves: sacred places of the Goddess, especially where sex magick is practiced.

Guardian: defender of spiritual wealth and power; guardian of the threshold between the conscious and subconscious minds. See **dwarf.**

Hair: lower types of energy in some cultures. In others, spiritual forces, psychic abilities. In yet others, fertility, the harvest, and strength. Some cultures believed that women could control winds, powers of creation, and magick by binding or loosing their hair; the goddess Isis was an example of this. Among the gods, such as Shiva, Apollo, and Herakles, long hair symbolized virility and power.

Halo: the successful rising of kundalini energy through the crown chakra. The halo is shown vividly in Hindu sculpture and art, and is also used commonly in Christian art.

Hand: related to the column and pillar. A symbol of support and strength, manifestation, and action. In the Orient, a hand combined with an eye symbolized clairvoyant ability. The blessing of an upraised hand with extended thumb and first two fingers was originally a Triple Goddess gesture of blessing.

Hare, rabbit: divination, fertility, creation, swiftness; a lunar animal. Known in many cultures around the world and generally associated with lunar goddesses.

Harp: the bridge between heaven and Earth; manifestation of the Will.

Harpies: negative aspects of spiritual or cosmic energy. Goddesses connected with Neptune and, originally, the sea; they were teachers who often posed riddles or the bearers of punishment.

Hat: thought, ideas.

Hawk: in Egypt, the soul; the vehicle for transformation. Connected with solar deities.

Head: thought that can change the world; Oneness. In some cultures, the abiding place of the soul; see **decapitation.** At Brauron, men who dedicated themselves to Artemis were given a cut on the neck, symbolic of ritual beheading.[17] The knighthood ceremony of touching the knight on the shoulder with a sword is a remnant of this.

Headache: problems; retribution for wrong actions.

Headdress and throne: in Mesopotamia, Babylon, and India, these refer to the Divine Center.

Heart: moral judgement; center of the physical life and symbol of eternity, as are all centers. The repository of the record of a human life. The only organ left by the Egyptians in the mummy.

Hearth: a type of domestic Sun; love, the home. Associated with the word Earth. In Greece and Rome, the center of family life; the hearth pit also was a communication point for the departed ancestors in the underworld.

Heat: sexual energy, creative fertility.

Heaven: communion with the deities, with the Divine; a state of spiritual bliss. Early cultures believed there was more than one heaven.

He-goat: a scapegoat; removal of sin or negativity. Uncontrolled sexuality, as with the god Pan.

Hell, The Pit, Tartarus: the deep areas of the subconscious where are hidden the problems we have refused to deal with. Reached by descending through the inner labyrinth.

Helmet: spiritual thoughts if the visor is up; hidden thoughts if the visor is down. The English word is derived from the goddess Hel, who often provided Her favored humans with the magickal Helkappe, or Cap of Darkness; this enabled them to be invisible while temporarily visiting Hel's land. When worn by deities, such as Athene, the helmet marked their divine status.

Herbs: natural forces, both good and evil, healing and destroying. Magickal energy available to humans.

Heron: generation of life. The ibis and stork have the same meaning.

Hippopotamus: strength, life; the Mother principle. The Egyptian goddess of birth was a hippo, Ta-Urt, who could also be a destroying aspect.

Hog, pig: low morals; allowing oneself to wallow in the physical senses. See **sow.**

Hole: regeneration; connected with the cave and cauldron. Naturally holed stones are still considered very lucky.

Honey: to the Greek Orphists, a symbol of wisdom. In India, the higher self. The seemingly miraculous product of a Goddess animal.

Hood: death which precedes regeneration; hidden motives.

Horns: originally a fertility and lunar symbol, as shown in the carving of the Great Goddess of Laussel holding Her horn with thirteen incisions on it. When used in connection with a goddess,[18] the balance of male and female, positive and negative energies in procreative action. When used with a god,[19] a sign of the Earth God; strength, power, male sexuality.

Horse: a variety of meanings, but often associated with death, the underworld, and ocean deities; vehicle for journeying to the underworld or land of the dead. Blind cosmic forces of chaos; forces of the physical world which can pull the body-chariot to ruin if not kept under

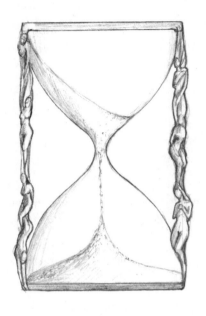

Hourglass

control. White horses are light, life, and positive energy; black ones darkness, death, and negative energy. The exception to this coloring was found in English and German folklore where dreaming of white horses meant death; Odin's grey horse, as part of the god's Wild Hunt, was a symbol of death.[20] The military funerals of today still put the boots backward in the stirrups, an ancient reminder of the idea that the feet of dead men are backward.

Horseshoe: a yonic emblem; the ending of one cycle and the beginning of another.

Hounds: our own subconscious judgement; companions, and also the terrifying form of the Maiden that drive us out of the labyrinth if we are unprepared. The name "bitches" was applied to the hunting priestesses of Diana.

Hourglass: the cycle and connection between the upper (spiritual) and lower (physical) worlds; creation and destruction.

House: similar in meaning to garden, chest, wall. The familiar area of life around each human.

Hunt, wild hunt: seeking which may have a destructive motive; when used in connection with a deity, the driving or forcing of a soul to a karmic end. Holda, Bertha.

Hunter, huntress: death, destruction, or forced transformation. A symbol applied to certain goddesses and gods. The protectress face of the Maiden. Artemis and Diana were known as Huntresses.

Ibis: as the bird of the Egyptian Thoth, symbolic of magick, spells, writing, and record-keeping. See **heron.**

Ice: transition between cycles, change in progress, the area of division between the conscious and subconscious minds; sometimes rigidity.

Imprison: to lock up anything is to halt progress; to bury experiences in order not to deal with them. The collective unconscious buried within the subconscious, and the subconscious within the conscious mind.

Incest: in myths a clue that matriarchal legends and stories were rewritten after a patriarchal takeover. Rape falls into the same category. Degradation, shame, the unspiritual enforcement of will over another.

Intestines: much the same as the labyrinth, maze, and the alchemical vessel called the alembic. Disintegration and the path back to the Great Goddess, whether physical, mental, or spiritual.

Intoxicated, drunk: filled with spiritual energy; this can be a negative experience if we are unprepared.

Invisibility: dissolution and sinking into the subconscious.

Island: a place set apart and secure; a spiritual sanctuary of the mind. In some cultures, a refuge; in others, such as the tale of Calypso, death, isolation, and solitude.

Jester: associated with the sign of Gemini. Duality, extreme opposites; the unpredictable qualities of Fate.

Jewels, gems: spiritual truths.

Journey: seeking, moving from one state of consciousness to another. Similar to flying, swimming, running. An initiation of some type.

Juice: similar to blood, wine, sacrifice.

Key: the means of solving a mystery or performing a task; symbols of locking and unlocking in magick, or binding and loosing.[21] Sometimes a potion is considered a key. Especially associated with Hecate and Persephone. The Egyptian ankh was considered a magickal key. Sophocles wrote of a key on the tongue in the Eleusinian Mysteries.

King: potential ruler over the conscious, subconscious, and collective unconscious minds.

Knife: vengeance, death, sacrifice; often the means of ending a cycle; magick and divination. The Celtic women of Ireland wore belt knives until the Christians made it illegal; however, a knife was part of a bride's costume until the seventeenth century.[22]

Knight: master over physical matter; the spiritual self which must gain control over the physical body, emotions, and mind.

Knot: stopping progress; binding up energies; sometimes complications or problems. Believed to control the weather, winds, birth, and death. See **curl.** Also having to do with the Fate goddesses and the human life threads. Mohammed once said that Jewish Witches almost killed him with a cord of knots.[23] The Flamen Dialis, high priest in Rome, was forbidden to wear any knot or even a closed ring for fear of binding his power.

Labyrinth, maze: the path leading back to the center; regeneration through the Great Mother. The labyrinth has a definite path; the maze doesn't. Campbell compares it to the intestines. The Egyptians had a labyrinth at Lake Moeris; the Cretans had two at Knossus; the Etruscans one at Clusium. Comparable to the life processes that led to and from the abyss.

Labrys, double axe: a Goddess and Moon symbol; said to have been one of the weapons preferred by the Amazons. A ceremonial scepter in Crete and at Delphi. Renewing of the life cycle and the soul through sacrifice.

Lake: similar to the sea and the cauldron. A symbol of the Goddess, it signified the land of the dead and the recreative powers of the spirit.

Lamp: spiritual intelligence and enlightenment, as in the myth of Psyche. Juno Lucina and Diana Lucifera were known as goddesses who brought light to the newborn. Ancient terra-cotta lamps in the shape of female genitals were mystical symbols of the sacred knowledge gained from the sexual priestesses of the Goddess.

Lantern: clue or guiding principle that leads one to the truth or spiritual enlightenment.

Leaf: to the Chinese, happiness. In other cultures, similar to herbs.

Leopard, tiger, panther: aggressiveness and power. The tiger was associated with Dionysus and was a symbol of cruelty. In China, the tiger symbolized the New Moon and darkness; to the Hindus, it was the uncontrolled base powers of the instincts.

Liberation: freeing the self or soul from entrapment in worldly ties; physical, mental, emotional, and spiritual independence.

Light: spirit; further, more specific meaning is derived from its color.

Lingam: integration of both sexes. A masculine symbol.

Lion: power and majesty; symbol of the Sun and the Earth. Associated with Cybele, Hathor, Sekhmet, Mehit, and other goddesses.

Loss: sacrifice before a purification.

Lotus, lily: spiritual purity, the heart and the sacred center, fertility. Sacred in Egypt and India. A symbol of the Universal Mother.

Magick, magick words: spiritual power molded into a desire or manifestation by following certain psychic laws; the words are often the power of our own will.

Lion

Maize: prosperity, fertility. In China, one of the eight emblems.

Mandrake: a number of meanings depending upon how the mandrake is used. The negative aspects of the soul; domination through the sexual urges; release of raw primitive emotions.

Man-eating monster: the destructive forces of the subconscious which can overcome and destroy if not properly controlled and used.

Marriage: joining of the positive/negative, male/female, conscious/subconscious for creative action.

Marsh, swamp: inability or unwillingness to make a decision.

Mask: a hidden metamorphosis; secrecy, hidden meanings. Often associated with shape-shifting, as implied in the Germanic Grimhelm,[24] or the temporary impersonation of deities. Cosmetics for the eyes used today is a faint form of this mask.

Minotaur: a half-man, half-bull monster; especially connected with the Cretan maze and the legend of Perseus and Ariadne. Partial evolution from the physical to the spiritual, with the physical and emotions still in control.

Mirror: a Goddess symbol connected with the Moon. Revealing of the truth; intuition and the psychic; the imagination. Soul-catchers or soul-carriers; Celtic women were buried with their mirrors which they believed carried their souls.[25] In India, the Great Goddess was called the Mirror of the Abyss. In one myth of Dionysus, the Titans were said to have caught the god's soul in a mirror. In medieval times, scribes believed that gazing into a mirror relieved tired eyes.

Mistletoe: regeneration; death followed by rebirth. Often associated with gods of the oak.

Moon: symbol of many goddesses, a few gods. Creation, ripeness, and destruction; cycles of life. Spiritual disciplines and initiations. The reflection and reflector of all planetary influences; the waxing and waning of influences. The crescent Moon was sometimes shown as horns.

Mother: the Goddess in Her second aspect which ranges from birthing to nurturing to terrible. The subconscious mind.

Mountain: gateway to the realm of spirit; similar to the world axis.

Mouth: a Mother symbol similar in meaning to cave or vaginal opening. Connected by the Egyptians to the creative Word. The Moslems have their women cover their faces because they equate the mouth with the vagina.

Mud: creative powers, biological processes.

Myths, stories, tales: maps to spiritual understanding of humankind's position in the universe.

Narcissus: self-contemplation, enamored with oneself, as in the tale of Narcissus. An innocent temptation which could lead to lack of freedom, as in the myth of Kore-Persephone.

Necklace: a symbol of the Goddess; also a sexual symbol of the vaginal opening like the mouth and circle. Emblems of Freyja and Ishtar. Unity of all things, a cosmic bond.

Nest: foundation.

Night: a feminine principle; the subconscious; the realm of the Goddess.

Nightmare: fear caused by images arising from the subconscious and collective unconscious minds. Demeter.

Nudity: a symbol of the unconcealed in spirit, but also signifying humankind's physical connections.

Numbers: numerology is in itself a complete study. However, it is said that odd numbers are sacred to the Goddess and even numbers to the God. The numbers three and nine were especially connected with the Triple Goddess. Thirteen was associated with the lunar months in a year and several goddesses, including Freyja. Three interlaced triangles, with a total of nine sides, represented the goddesses of Fate and the Celtic nine Morrigans. In Nordic tradition, the sign of fate was the Knot of Vala (priestess and seeress), the valknut, [26] again a twining of three triangles. The Greek body, mind, and shade was the origin for the later Christian body, mind, and spirit; the Asians and Hebrews had similar definitions.[27] Multiples of three were said to increase power. The number six was a sexual number, sacred to Aphrodite.

Nymphs: Water elementals who controlled birth, fertility, dissolution, and death; the Greek word means both bride and doll. Entities who are fluid in nature and appearance and who live in both the physical and astral realms.

Oak: strength and long life. Sacred to Cybele, Jupiter, and Thorr. In Greek-Roman tradition, the oak symbolized the goddess Diana and Her King of the Wood; in England, it was associated with Herne the Hunter, Lord of the Forest.

Oar: controlling the direction life is taking; stability within an unstable situation.

Ocean: the source of life; the creative matrix where the formed arises from the formless; the subconscious, spirit. Originally the province of the Great Mother; later usurped by Neptune, Poseidon, and other gods. In a little-known Greek myth, the goddess Eurynome created the sea god Oceanus, a serpent-figure associated with the Great Goddess. Because Oceanus was shown holding his tail in his mouth, he can be compared with the Gnostic Ouroboros.

Octagon: intermediate between a circle and a square. Can have either eight or twelve sides. Spiritual regeneration by combining of the positive and negative.

Octopus: similar to the spider and cobweb. Unfolding of the creative-destructive processes.

Ogre: the masculine principle when it works against the feminine principle. Perhaps a later interpretation of Cronus devouring his children as soon as they were born.

Old man, old woman: age-old wisdom; the collective unconscious. In particular, the old woman refers to the Crone aspect of the Goddess.

Oven, furnace: a symbol of the Great Mother and Her creative energies.

Owl: more than one meaning. To the Egyptians, a symbol of death, night, and cold. To the Greeks, an emblem of wisdom and the goddess Athene. The Moon, lunar mysteries, initiations. Its staring eyes connect it with the Eye Goddess, Lilith, Athene, Minerva, Blodeuwedd, Anath, and Mari.

Ox: in Egypt and India, symbolic of suffering, sacrifice, labor, patience. In Greece and Rome, seen as a lunar animal; the Earth Mother, sacrifice, triumph.

Palace, castle: a sacred place; the Divine Center.

Pentagram

Papyri, book: an unfolding of life; the Akashic Records, or the records of each person's many lives.

Peaches: to the Asians, immortality as with the apples.

Peacock: associated with various goddesses, such as Hera and Sarasvati. The iridescent colors and "eyes" symbolize watchfulness and divine justice.

Pearl: one of the eight Chinese emblems. To the Moslems, the symbol of heaven. The sacred center.

Pegasus: converting evil into good. The winged horse that sprang from the blood of Medusa when Perseus cut off Her head; another clue to a rewritten myth.

Pentacle, pentagram: five-point star with one point up; symbol of the Goddess in all Her forms. In ancient Egypt, it was the star of Isis and Nephthys; in the Middle East, that of Ishtar. To the Celts it was the sign the Morrigan. A sign of the Earth Element in Tarot. This symbol can be seen in an apple by cutting it crosswise. Repulsion of evil; protection.

Perfume: memories.

Petrification: detain, enclose, stop evolution on all levels.

Phallus, penis: symbol of the male principle's part in the act of creation. See **lingam.**

Phoenix: reincarnation, rebirth, regeneration. A symbol of the Sun gods.

Pilgrim: the seeker after new and perhaps hidden knowledge; one who journeys through the labyrinth. See **journey** and **labyrinth.**

Pillar: see **column.**

Pine tree, evergreens: immortality. The cones are fertility symbols.

Plait, braid: intertwining of relationships, creative matter, or consciousness. One form, the double helix, is the matrix of all matter. Sometimes means binding and unbinding, as in magick done with knots and ropes.

Planets: different cosmic energies. The seven planets known to the ancients correspond to the seven directions of space: Earth is considered the center, the Sun the zenith, the Moon the nadir, the rest the typical four directions known on Earth. Gods and goddesses in nearly every culture have been connected with the planets.

Plow: delving into the deeper areas of consciousness. Since the Earth is considered female, plowing signifies the union of the male and female, whether in spiritual principle or physical actuality. Gefion.

Pomegranate: a fruit connected with the underworld queen Persephone and called food of the dead. The Greeks believed it sprang from the blood of Dionysus, similar in idea to the anemone and Adonis and the violet and Attis. The pomegranate with its many chambers and seeds symbolizes the dead lying in sleep until they are reborn from the underworld, or Oneness within the recycling Dark Mother.

Potion: menstrual blood; drink of immortality, particularly applied to women in myths this way; the proper key. Known to the Hindus as *soma*, the Persians as *haoma*, and the Celts as red claret. Also related to the geas, a very common occurrence among the ancient Celts.[28] An uncontrollable, compelling force that draws one toward a karmic destiny. Sometimes this happens when we refuse to face a situation or deal with a problem; we are then drawn back into similar situations or problems until we make the correct decisions. Drinking the potion can mean either following the pull of the geas or listening to the intuitive, psychic knowing that comes from within. Ch'ang-O.

Pregnant: period of time while an idea or desire develops. A time of rest before completion of projects.

Prince: son of a king, and therefore the reborn son/lover consort of the Mother; the future challenger of the sacrificial king.

Procession, marching: connected with the pilgrim and the labyrinth. See **journey.** Sometimes a deliberate magickal journeying into the depths of the subconscious and collective unconscious minds. Clockwise processions are for creative energy-building; counterclockwise for dissipation.

Prophecy: spiritual wisdom; warning; advice given by the deities through a human.

Pumpkin: a link between two worlds; an upheaval of the usual order, as in the story of Cinderella.

Putrefication, rot: black crows, skeletons, skulls, and other funeral signs fall into this category; all symbols of the underworld queen, the Dark Mother. Regeneration arising out of physical or symbolic destruction.

Pyramid: the hollow ones and those with three sides (making a multiple of three) are symbols of the Great Mother and rebirth through Her. They are connected with the Element of Fire and the cosmic Fire or Light that is necessary for regeneration and creation. The solid pyramids and those with four sides are symbols of physical matter and the Great Father.

Queen: high priestess of the Goddess; a sacred marriage with her conferred the right to rule.

Rags and tatters: wounds in the soul.

Rain: spiritual fertilization of life; spiritual influences upon the Earth.

Rats: infirmity and death; associated with plagues, which are one of the Mother's ways of correcting imbalances.

Raven: messenger from spirit or the dead; oracles and teachers of magick. Sacred to the Celtic Rhiannon and the Morrigan. Among the Native Americans of the Northwest, the Siberians, and Innuit, Raven was an important god married to the Great Mother.

Rectangle: contained and controlled security, stability, power.

Reefs, shoals: obstacles to destiny, as in the story of Circe in the *Odyssey*.

Regard, glance: defense, protection of the body, mind, and soul. In later cultures this changed into cursing, when people were thought to have the Evil Eye.

Reins: willpower; the connection and relationship between the body and soul.

Return: reintegration of the spirit with the Great Mother.

Ring: continuity, wholeness; the eternally repeated cycle of time. A symbol of the female vaginal opening; three rings represented the Triple Goddess. In folklore rings are often connected with magick charms. Three joined rings were used in ancient traditions to invoke the three Fates.[29]

Rite, ritual: rhythmic movement of the astral; passage of time. When power or energy is used from the astral planes to mold a desire in the physical. Contact with deities within a consecrated magickal circle. A set of repeated actions, usually of a spiritual or magickal nature.

River: fertile, creative power of time and Nature.

Rose

Rock: stability, permanence. Sometimes a barrier.

Room: private thoughts with windows of understanding. Without windows, a closed mind.

Rope: for binding; similar to knots and curls.

Rose: achievement and perfection. The color may change its meaning. Connected with many goddesses, such as Aphrodite, Cybele, and the Babylonian Gula. The five-petaled rose is another form of pentacle.

Rotation: generation of magickal force or creative power, as with the spiral or circular processions. Rotation clockwise builds up positive or creating energy; counterclockwise, negative or dissipating energy.

Round table: connected with the sky or spiritual realms. The twelve knights of Arthur's legend symbolized the signs of the Zodiac.

Rudder: safety and guidance.

Ruins: desolation and death.

Sacrifice: the giving up of something, even personal habits, in order to gain spiritual energy to create a transformation in matter or thought. Paying for mistakes.

Sails: creative breath, action, the Element of Air.

Salamander: connected with the Element of Fire; fire-energy of spirit.

Sandals, winged: methods of reaching the higher areas of spirit; a symbol of Mercury. Similar to Pegasus.

Sarcophagus, coffin: a feminine symbol of the beginning and ending of material life through the womb-tomb of the Dark Mother.

Scales: justice; cause and effect; divine assessment of a life. Maat, Astraea.

Scepter: fertility, purification, the ability and willpower to make changes. Related to the magick wand, the thunderbolt, the phallus, and Thorr's hammer.

Scissors: an emblem of the Fate spinners who cut the life-thread to the correct length. A symbol of both life and death.

Scythe: the harvest when the life-path is finished. Shown in every size from the large agricultural tool to the small hand-held implement. Connected with Rhea, Gaea, Artemis, and Cybele. The shape is symbolic of the Moon. The Grim Reaper of the current New Year's celebration is an adaptation of the scythe-carrying Crone. See **mask.**

Sea: the source of all life; associated with the Great Mother and Her re-creating cauldron.

Seal of Solomon: two interlacing triangles; the downward-pointing female merging with the upward-pointing male. The human soul which benefits only when the conscious and subconscious minds are joined.

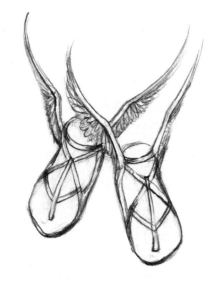

Winged sandals

Secret: deep spiritual mysteries whose answers never remain the same and which can be disclosed only through communion with the Goddess.

Serpent, snake: pure divine energy; beginning and ending; the kundalini. Intertwined snakes, usually around a central staff, were a sign of healing. An animal sacred to the Goddess in particular; several gods use this symbol, showing that they took over their functions from a goddess. The Python of Delphi was a son/consort of the Goddess; the priestesses there were called Pythonesses. The Egyptian goddess Ua Zit or Buto was called the Serpent Mother; Her hieroglyphic sign was the uraeus or cobra.

Shadow: the astral body; the alter ego of the soul. In some myths, this is portrayed as a negative entity, composed of all the hidden habits and desires of a person. The seven souls of ancient Egypt included the *khaibut* or shadow; the Greek and Roman shade (*umbra*) was the part of the soul that went to the underworld. At one time the saying "to lose one's shadow" meant to lose the soul.

Shape-shifter: changing of form or the personality that one presents to the world. Shape-shifting goddesses include Artemis and Flidhais.

Sheaf: unification, strength, but also limitation from the binding.

Shell: symbol of the Great Mother since one of Her original provinces was the sea from which the shells come. One of the eight emblems of ancient China. Related to the Moon, the feminine principle, and women. The spiraled ones are particularly symbolic of the life force continuing from one generation to another.

Shield: protection, but also identity, as with the knights who displayed their personal emblems on their shields.

Ship: the journey through life in a physical sense, or the inner journey in a spiritual sense. The type and condition of the ship is determined by whether one decides to live for oneself totally or to help others.

Sickle: the Moon and its influences on humans.

Sieve: sorting out, purifying, discarding the useless.

Siren: temptation to leave the true path. Either a bird-woman or a fish-woman; the Greek sirens were the daughters of the nymph Calliope whom Ceres turned into birds.

Skeleton: death and disintegration; the bare bones of a matter or problem.

Spider

Skin: birth and rebirth; in Egyptian hieroglyphics, three skins knotted together symbolized being born. Vulnerability, as when naked.

Skull: in a wide sense, human mortality, as in *Hamlet* and *Faust*. To other cultures, it symbolized the surviving part of humans (the soul) when the body was destroyed.

Sleeping Beauty: the awakening of any person asleep unnaturally, such as Brynhild in Germanic myth. The dormant subconscious before it becomes stimulated and active.

Smoke: in some cultures, the magickal ability to ward off ill-fortune; in others, a signpost leading to spiritual knowledge.

Snail: the action of the primordial spiral of energy upon matter; this applies to all spiraling shells. This action, particularly when applied to magickal spells, may appear to work slowly, as in the snail's movement, but is steady and progressive.

Sorcerer: the Terrible Father, as in Saturn and certain aspects of other gods. Conflict between the female and male principles.

Sow: magick, the underworld, deep knowledge of the Crone. A lunar Goddess animal; associated with Astarte, Cerridwen, Demeter, Freyja, and the Buddhist Marici.

Space: the realm between chaos and the cosmos; the place where time comes into existence.

Sphinx: multiplicity and fragmentation of the cosmos, or the actions of the Dark Mother. Bast, in Her form as Pasht, was known as the devouring Sphinx.

Spin: to create destiny and time. Creation of karma.

Spider: creation; the spiraling energy of primordial matter; the Divine Center in the web of illusion (as in India); the eternal creation and destruction by the Goddess. A symbol of the Crone aspect and the Fates. A Pueblo myth tells of Spider Woman who spins the universe into being; She also created the Sun and Moon and all four colors of humans. Spider Grandmother of the Kiowa is similar; in Ghana, Anansi is the Spider Goddess.

Spindle: temporal life; the generating forces of the universe. In relating to the Moon, the transitory phases of humans. Connected with Ishtar and the Fates.

Springs, wells, rivers: the Earth's blood; fertility, growth, purity.

Spiral: evolution of the universe; the constantly moving energies of creation-destruction; primordial matter of the Great Mother; path to the land of the dead. Also symbolic of the labyrinth or maze that leads to the Divine Center. Dances that spiral inward then outward represent the labyrinthlike path of death and rebirth. In Sumeria, spirals were symbols of the sacred serpent guardians of the temples.

Spur: similar to winged sandals.

Spying: to gain knowledge not intended for you.

Square: symbolic of the four Elements. Definition, stability, firmness; linear thinking without intuition. A masculine symbol.

Staff: support, authority; sometimes punishment.

Stag: similar to the Tree of Life because of the branching antlers; an animal of the Great God or Lord of the Forest. Sometimes an emblem of the sacrificial son/lover of the Great Mother. The animal passions and mentality.

Star: spirit shining in the darkness of the labyrinth; a beacon to guide the pilgrim on the journey through the subconscious. See **pentacle.** Sometimes the astral body.

Steps: communication between different levels of mind and different worlds.

Stork: a messenger of new ideas. When used in connection with the goddess Juno, a symbol of filial devotion.

Stone: the dwelling place of primordial power; god/dess power. Before humans began to carve images to represent their deities, they held certain stones in reverence. Pausanias wrote that the very old Roman Graces were based on the Triple Goddess; at Orchomenos their symbol was three standing stones.[30] In Iceland the goddess Armathr, deity of prosperity, was represented by a certain stone.[31] In certain parts of Europe, holed stones are still used as conception charms.[32] At one time certain Arabs called themselves Beni Sahr, sons of the Rock. The Hag of Scone, now called the Stone of Scone, rests under the British coronation throne in Westminster Abbey; the function of this stone is very similar to the Stone of Fail in Irish mythology, which was the choosing and consecration of the ruler by the Goddess. In ancient Rome, the Tarpeian Rock on Capitoline Hill originally was made sacred by an Etruscan goddess.

Storm: the wild primitive emotions usually kept under control in the subconscious; sometimes creative combining of the Elements. Unpleasant lessons of life and their consequences.

Stranger: the possibility of unforeseen change; sometimes a spiritual messenger or teacher.

Sun: the creative, yet also destructive, power of prime matter. The heart of spirit; spiritual power; too much Sun is an overdose of spirit. A few cultures, such as Japan and Germany, had Sun goddesses. The masculine principle and emblem of the Sun god.

Swallow: the bird is spring, the growth of Nature; sacred to Venus and Isis. To swallow something is to try to hide it or un-know it.

Swan: satisfaction of a desire; messengers from the Goddess. Sacred to Aphrodite, Venus, and Sarasvati. Swan Maidens are well-known in Indo-European myths; the Valkyries wore swan-feather cloaks on occasion.

Swastika: the solar wheel of the year or seasons; movement of time. Similar to the cross.

Sword: the power to wound or liberate; strength, defense. In many ways similar to the cross because of its shape.

Tattoo: sacrifice through the flow of blood; according to the design, often a warding or banishing device.

Teeth: protection, attack, activity. Loss of teeth symbolizes castration, failure in life. The ancient idea of being marked by teeth of the spirit implies the opening of prophetic abilities.

Temple: a sacred place; the Divine Center within the subconscious, the doorway to the collective unconscious.

Thirst: a blind appetite for life.

Thorn: a conjunction between existence and non-existence, joy and agony. Associated with the Egyptian goddess Neith; related to the world tree and the cross.

Thread: the connection between the physical body and the soul; the Christians called this the Silver Cord, but other religions said it was golden or red. Sometimes a guiding marker through the inner labyrinth. Ariadne.

Threshold: the doorway to transition; the connection between the conscious and subconscious minds, protected by the inner guardian who repels all who are not prepared. The Roman god Janus with two faces symbolizes this guardian.

Throne: stability and unity to the Asians; to the Egyptians, support, security, and exaltation.

Tower

Thunderbolt: celestial fire, terrible but dynamic; illumination, chance, destiny. Most commonly the scepter-emblem of a sky god, such as Zeus, Jupiter, Shiva, Keraunos, Pyerun, Thorr, and others. The Oriental *dorje* and the trident are forms of the thunderbolt.

Titans: untamable forces of primeval Nature; wild, uncontrolled energies issuing forth from chaos; the raw primitive emotions of humankind.

Tomb: womb symbol of the Dark Mother; also of the resting period of the dense-matter body while it undergoes transformation; the subconscious.

Torch: truth, purification through spiritual illumination. An emblem of the goddess Cybele.

Tower: rising above the physical; ascent of the spirit; sometimes the overblown ego of humans before a fall.

Toys: temptation, such as when the Titans offered toys to the baby Dionysus.

Treasure: knowledge and mysteries of life and spirit found within the subconscious and collective unconscious realms. This knowledge is dispensed at the discretion of the Mother and the Crone.

Triangle: associated with the number three; emblem of the Triple Goddess. With the apex downward, a sign for woman; upward, a masculine symbol. The three in one unity of the Goddess.[33] It was the sign of motherhood, the Moon, and the female principle in Egypt. The Arabs believed that the triangle represented three Moon goddesses: Al-Uzza, Manat, and Al-Lat. A motif of three triangles, often interlaced, was the symbol of the Fate goddesses, such as the Greek Moerae, the Nordic Norns, the Roman Fortunae, and the later medieval Parcae. The Triple Goddess was also revered by the Christian Gnostics,[34] which was one of the reasons the sect was outlawed and persecuted by the other Christians. In earliest India, the Triple Goddess was called Trimurti, or Trinity. Later, three gods took over the title, but the goddess Parashakti still was symbolized by a triangle with three seeds within it.[35]

Trident: a sexual symbol of the prowess needed by the god who fertilizes the Triple Goddess; associated with Neptune. A tripling of force.

Triform: spiritual knowledge, science, armed might; body, mind, spirit; creation, preservation, destruction. Another name for Hecate; could also be applied to the Celtic Morrigan.

Tripod: similar to the triangle, the Trinity, and the number three. This was an early Greek form of the outdoor sacrificial altar because the tripod was more stable on uneven ground. There was a street in Athens leading to the temple of Dionysus which was called the Street of Tripods; it came by this name because it was lined with a multitude of such small altars.

Trumpet: fame and glory; warning. Associated with the Elements of Fire and Air.

Tunic: the self; the projected mask of identity we show to others.

Turtle: in the Far East, the cosmos; in Nigeria, the female sex organs; in alchemy, primordial matter. Not creative forces, but the seeds of unformed matter which will be manifested.

Twilight: the half-light of morning or evening; the dividing line which joins but also keeps separate opposing forces.

Twins: sometimes a doubling of power; other times opposites, such as life and death.

Underworld: see **hell.**

Underworld demons: dark karmic currents which often propel a person to follow a destructive path; this usually occurs when a person has mentally refused to face needed changes in life. Symbolic of the death-wish, especially prevalent in heroes of folk tales. In myths these demons were such as the Greek harpies and Erinyes, the Hindu Rakshasas, Arabian djinns, and the Norse-Germanic Valkyries and dark elves.

Undines: feminine spirits or entities of the Element of Water. The nega-tive and sometimes unpredictable emotions that can arise from the influence of the Moon.

Unicorn: chastity, purity; known in a vast array of cultures, including the Indian Vedas.

Urn: a womb symbol; a feminine-principle container; Oneness which proceeds from the Mother. One of the Chinese eight emblems of good luck.

Valley: a neutral area for creation and manifestation in the material world. The Wiccan consecrated circle, Pagan temples, and sacred places fall into this category.

Vase: similar to the urn; repose and fertility. In Egypt, a sign of the god-dess Nu. The pre-Hellenic goddess Pandora the All-Giver[36] has a huge vase as Her symbol.

Vault: beginning in prehistoric times, this represented the union of the sky god and the Earth goddess. A contained safe place for creating and storing energy.

Vine: connected to grapes. From the earliest times, a symbol of the Great Mother, sacrifice, and fecundity.

Volcano: the potential for self-destruction; violence which can affect others. In some cultures, the outward sign of evil; in others, anti-thetical powers. Underworld deities, such as Vulcan, were associated with volcanoes; on the Pacific islands, goddesses such as Pele and Fuji are connected with volcanoes.

Vomit: to bring something forth in a new cycle.

Vulture: spiritual counsel; destruction followed by rebirth. In Egypt, a symbol of the Great Mother and Her destructive/regenerative pow-ers. In India, individual guides and guardians. In Egypt the hiero-glyph for "mother" was a vulture; the mother of Egypt, Nekhbet or Mut, was often shown in vulture form.

Wand, magick: see **scepter.**

War: the struggle of light against dark, good against evil. This is seen in such myths as Jupiter against the Titans and Thorr against the Giants.

Warrioress: the woman and mother's fighting instinct to preserve her off-spring and family.

Warriors: ancestors; if hostile, antagonistic forces; if protective, latent forces that can come to the aid of the consciousness.

Water: primal matter; universal possibilities. A symbol of the Great Mother and Her creative forces.

Waves: movement of forms being created within primal matter. The Chinese believed that dragons lived in waves.

Weaving: the life of an individual. Emblem of the Fates and other such deities, particularly female, who dealt with human lives and karma. Also the creating of magick.

Well: purification and healing. Associated with Demeter and Brigit. Wells of all kinds were at one time guarded and served by priestesses; making a wish and casting in a coin was a form of prayer to the goddess of the well.

West: land of the dead where the spirit returns to the Goddess for recycling. To the Egyptians and Greeks, the place of spirits. To the Nordic peoples, the place of a poisoned sea of destruction and an abyss. The Welsh Celts told of the Western Isles of Paradise.

Whale: interaction of the world, the body, and the grave. Embracing opposites of existence, as the whale within the sea. Being swallowed by a whale symbolizes a ritual death during initiation which leads to a rebirth.

Wheel: spiritual advancement or regression, depending upon whether the wheel is turning clockwise or counterclockwise. A Sun symbol. Time and the movement of karma.

Wild animals: unknown qualities of the subconscious mind.

Whip: domination, mastery, punishment.

Whirlwind: universal evolution.

Wind: the violent and active aspects of the Element of Air. In Arabic and Hebrew, it means both breath and spirit. The Greeks associated it with the destructive god Typhon.

Window: symbolic of eyes, which have been called windows of the soul.

Witch

Wine: blood and sacrifice; youth and eternal life; sometimes abandonment of inhibitions and/or self-control. Associated with the god Dionysus.

Wine skin: the Greek expression "to untie the wine skin" meant to indulge in sexual pleasures.

Wings: spirituality, imagination, mobility, enlightenment, rising of the spiritual thought. Love and victory to the Greeks, as seen in their winged deities Athene, Artemis, and Aphrodite.[37]

Witch: the picture which has come down to us is usually of an old, evil, ugly woman, but that is a patriarchal view of the original Crone. Time, deep power from the dark void.

Wolf: strength, cunning, intelligence. To the Egyptians and Romans, valor. Among the Norse, the destructive powers of chaos which will eventually reclaim all matter. The expression "a wolf in sheep's clothing" probably originated with the shape-shifting abilities and astral travels of priestesses and shamans. The Goddess as a wolf was associated with the Roman Lupa or Feronia and the Vestal Virgins.

Wood: burned, it signifies wisdom, death, and return to the Mother through cremation. Green wood is a sign of fertility.

Woodlands: see **forest.**

Worm: a creative symbol which first kills, then destroys before the basic building blocks can be formed into new matter.

Year: all cyclic processes and rhythms; evolution and involution; cause and effect.

Yoke: union and discipline; accepting of responsibilities. Sacrifice because of its association with the ox.

ENDNOTES

PART I

Chapter 1

1. M. Esther Harding, in *Woman's Mysteries: Ancient and Modern*, has written extensively on this from a Jungian point of view.

2. Pythagoras lived in the sixth century BCE and became known as the Father of Numbers. His teachings were based on mathematics, music, and astronomy, the Triangular Foundation of all the arts and sciences.

3. Corrine Heline, *Sacred Science of Numbers*.

4. Florence Campbell in *Your Days Are Numbered* writes that the science of numbers began to be used more than 11,000 years ago and clues point to perhaps twice that long. The Egyptian Ritual of the Dead, the Indian Vedas, the Chinese Circle of the Heavens, and the Hebrew Qabala all deal in one way or another with numerology.

Chapter 2

1. Carl G. Jung, *The Archetypes and the Collective Unconscious*.

2. The collective unconscious, a term used by Jung, has also been referred to by some writers as the superconscious or the race mind. To me, the term race mind is far too limiting a title to apply to this vast reservoir of knowledge. Inherited racial memories are part of the collective unconscious, but this part of the mind goes far beyond the narrow scope of individual races.

It appears to be a receptacle for universal knowledge and understanding, surpassing individual, national, or racial inheritance. Jung dealt with this in detail in his *The Archetypes and the Collective Unconscious*.

3. Mircea Eliade, *Myths, Dreams and Mysteries*.

4. Jean Shinoda Bolen has two books, *Goddesses in Every Woman* and *Gods in Every Man*, which deal entirely with this subject.

Chapter 3

1. BCE means Before Common Era, or before the year AD 1 decided upon by the Christians. I have no quarrel with the dating; after all, dating must start somewhere. Many people do, however, dislike using the designations BC and AD since that implies a belief in Christianity. To accommodate all the religious beliefs in the world it seems more equitable to use BCE and CE (Common Era), which have nothing to do with any particular religion.

2. Riane Eisler, *The Chalice and the Blade*.

3. Marija Gimbutas, *The Goddesses and Gods of Old Europe*. Also her book *The Language of the Goddess*.

4. Starhawk, *The Spiral Dance*.

5. Anton Ehrenzweig, *The Hidden Order of Art*.

PART II

Chapter 5

1. Rex Warner, in *The Stories of the Greeks*, gives the Roman version of the story of Ceres (Demeter) and Proserpina (Persephone), who was called Kore before Her journey to the underworld.

2. *Lost Goddesses of Early Greece: A Collection of Pre-Hellenic Myths*.

3. The Mysteries were open to men, women, children, or slaves if they spoke Greek and had not killed another person. If the candidate had killed someone, the offender had to be ritually purified and expiated of the death. Demetra George, *Mysteries of the Dark Moon*.

4. It was said that initiation into the Deeper Mysteries granted the initiates immortality only if they kept the oath of silence. To this day there are no records of exactly what went on during certain parts of these rituals. The Lesser Eleusinia, February 1-3, celebrated Persephone's return from the underworld; this was open to all people, not just initiates. The Greater Eleusinia, September 23-October 1, celebrated the descent of Kore, and was for initiates only. For more information, see the chapter on Greece in *The Ancient and Shining Ones*.

5. Roman mythology says that the Vestal Virgin Rhea Silvia was raped by the god Mars and became the mother of Romulus and Remus, who founded Rome. Norma Lorre Goodrich, *Priestesses*.

6. She was worshipped first at every feast by the Romans.

7. W. R. Lethaby, *Architecture, Mysticism and Myth*.

8. The word "hearth" probably came from Earth.

9. The Amazons were loyal to Her aspect as the New Moon. In Ephesus, She was called Dea Anna, "the many-breasted," and Her Ephesian statues portray this.

10. The Greeks used the name Alani for the Scythian tribes who worshipped this goddess. Her hunting priestesses were considered to be sacred bitches. In the myth of the goddess and Actaeon, Her hounds were called Alani.

11. The Russians called wormwood a cursed herb because it was sacred to the Vilas (Pagan nymphs). But wormwood also is credited with protective powers.

12. Barbara Walker in *The Woman's Encyclopedia of Myths and Secrets* says that Actaeon's being changed into a stag designated him as the stag king who ruled for half a year, then was sacrificed. Artemis did have a male companion, Orion, a hunter-friend (stag king?) who was accidentally shot by the goddess. Actaeon appears to be another form of the forest god Cernunnos.

13. This punishment may be similar to the blindness that fell on Peeping Tom during Lady Godiva's ride. Some rituals of the Goddess were to be seen only by women. Any men who spied upon them and were caught were punished, usually torn to pieces by the worshipping women.

14. Other names under which She was known were Dione, Nemorensis, and Nemetona (Goddess of the Moongrove). Dione was originally the oracle-goddess at the shrine of Dodona before it was taken over by Zeus. In Italy, the woodland lake of Nemi in a volcanic crater in the Alban Hills held a woodland sanctuary dedicated to Diana. Her reigning priest there was called the King of the Wood and held his post by right of combat. Any man, free or slave, could challenge him.

15. As Moon goddess, Diana was shown with a crescent Moon rising above Her forehead. Max J. Herzberg, *Myths and Their Meaning*.

16. Charles Mills Gayley, *The Classic Myths in English Literature and Art*.

17. The herb dittany of Crete, the Greek name being *diktamnon*, was sacred to Dictynna. Its magickal qualities are the ability to reveal to the physical senses any spirits that may be near.

18. Anne Baring and Jules Cashford, *The Myth of the Goddess*, write that the Ephesian spring festival included a bullfight similar to that once held in Minoa or Crete.

19. Also called Bona Dea (Good Goddess, only worshipped by women) and closely related to Maia.

20. Menrva was Her Etruscan name. The Roman Mensa, goddess of numbers, calendars, measurements, and record-keeping, may have been an older title of Minerva as the Moon, or measurer of women's menses.

21. The owl, because of its staring eyes, may have been another symbol of the Eye Goddess of the Mediterranean. The owl was also sacred to Lilith, Blodeuwedd, Anath, and several other goddesses, all connected with the Moon. Neumann, in *The Great Mother*, points out that there were thousands of Eye Goddess images found around the ancient matriarchal city of Mari.

22. The Gorgons were originally a triad of Medusa, Stheino, and Euryale.

23. Ganymede's supplanting of Hebe is likely another patriarchal attempt to usurp a goddess's position of power in the minds of the people.

24. Alexander S. Murray, *Who's Who in Mythology*.

25. The name Maat may be based on the Indo-European word Ma, which means mother. She was known both in Sumeria and by the African Pygmies as Matu, the mother of God.

26. E. A. Wallis Budge, *The Gods of the Egyptians*.

27. Other Egyptian goddesses were also associated with the feather or plume. Budge, *The Gods of the Egyptians*.

28. Merlin Stone, *Ancient Mirrors of Womanhood*.

29. Barbara Mertz, *Temples, Tombs and Hieroglyphs*.

30. Pronounced "night."

31. The idea of cats having nine lives may have come from Artemis being considered the head of the nine Muses. Black cats were especially sacred to Bast and their symbol was displayed for healers. To kill a cat in Egypt was to be sentenced to death. Bast had a cat head and carried a sistrum.

32. In Her destroying aspect She was known as Pasht, the Tearer or devouring Sphinx.

33. It was an ancient matriarchal belief that the mother caused a child's soul to enter its body at birth. The soul-name was kept secret so that charms and spells could not be worked by its usage.

34. Charles Squire, *Celtic Myth and Legend*.

35. It was not unusual to find goddesses in threes or multiples of three, as their powers were said to increase by this multiplication.

36. Jeffrey Gantz, trans., *The Mabinogion*, and Charles Squire, *Celtic Myth and Legend*.

37. Lleu's death by a spear thrust into his side is in the same pattern as other sacrificed gods such as Balder and Krishna. Tradition says that Lleu rose again the next year to challenge Gronw.

38. An older version of this myth says that Gwydion chased Her through the sky, the Milky Way being the remains of this hunt. The owl was said to be a bird of wisdom and lunar mysteries; these birds either accompanied or represented such goddesses as Athene and Lilith.

39. Robert Graves, *The Greek Myths*.

40. Rufus and Lawson, in *Goddess Sites: Europe,* write that Kildare was anglicized from Cill Dara, the place of the oak.

41. It is possible that the name Kelly or Kelley came from this ancient Celtic word. Originally, the name *kelle* probably came from the eastern goddess Kali, since the Celtic Brigit was associated also with the three colors (white, red, and black) called gunas in India and representing Kali's power of creation, preservation, and destruction.

42. She was said to often appear as a hind or doe, leading heroes on adventures of mystical value. The Norse knew Her, saying that when these heroes died She took them to Hinderfjall, or Hind Mountain (Turville-Petrie, *Myth and Religion of the North*).

43. The Christian word Easter and the springtime date of this festival came from this goddess's worship. Even the image of the Easter bunny came from the goddess's Moon hare, sacred in many Eastern and Western cultures.

44. Norma Lorre Goodrich, *Medieval Myths*.

45. *New Larousse Encyclopedia of Mythology*.

46. Magick can be defined as magickal ritual, prayers, meditation, and other endeavors. For a more complete discussion on magick and how it works, see *Celtic Magic* and *Norse Magic*.

47. The Celts had a spiritual island paradise called Avalon, or Apple-isle, where they said the apples of immortality were kept.

48. Snorri Sturluson, *The Prose Edda*.

49. The Norse believed that apples, as a symbol or actuality, were vital to rebirth; Lee Hollander, *The Skalds*. In the legend of Sigurd (Siegfried), his great-grandmother conceived when she ate an apple; E. O. G. Turville-Petrie, *Myth and Religion of the North*.

50. Charles Squire, *Celtic Myth and Legend*.

51. This drink of immortality may well be the menstrual blood that is influenced by the Moon. The red claret of the fairy queen mentioned in Celtic myth alludes to menstrual fluid also.

52. Later, patriarchy diabolized this goddess into the patroness of whores. Robert Briffault, *The Mothers*.

53. The Norse knew Her as Luna, or Moon Shining on the Sea.

54. *New Larousse Encyclopedia of Mythology*.

PART III

Chapter 6

1. The Empress card of the Tarot is an excellent visual and symbolic example of this.

Chapter 7

1. Joseph Campbell, *The Masks of God: Creative Mythology*.

2. Robert Briffault, *The Mothers*.

3. Joseph Campbell, *The Masks of God: Oriental Mythology*.

4. Delphi means "womb." It was Greece's oldest and best known oracle site. Walker and Graves say that Mother Earth was worshipped there under the title of Delphyne, the Womb of Creation. This Mother's consort/son was the serpent Python, killed by Apollo. This accounts for the priestesses there being called Pythonesses. The Greeks called Delphi the Temple of the Womb and placed the world's navel at that spot; the omphalos stone was the symbol of this navel.

5. In 395 CE, fanatical Christian monks destroyed the temple at Eleusis because of the sexual implications of some of the rituals. But they could not stop the people's devotion to Demeter or the continuation of Her ceremonies for a few more centuries.

6. S. Angus, *The Mystery-Religions*.

7. In Sanskrit the word "de" is *dwr* and in Celtic *duir*. In the Hebrew Qabalistic Tree of Life the sign of daleth means the door of birth and death.

8. J. J. Bachofen, *Myth, Religion, and Mother Right*.

9. Robert Graves, *The Greek Myths*.

10. Since this was often called supernatural red wine, it is quite likely a metaphor for menstrual blood; it granted the gods immortality. The same symbol occurs in the Vedas under the name of *soma*, in Persia *haoma*, and in Egypt *sa*. It is always associated with the Moon. See R. Graves, *The Greek Myths*; Budge, *The Gods of the Egyptians*.

11. Maarten J. Vermaseren, *Cybele and Attis*.

12. The word "rejuvenate" probably comes from the name of this goddess.

13. J. J. Bachofen, *Myth, Religion, and Mother Right*.

14. E. A. Wallis Budge in *Egyptian Magic* writes that the Christians stole the phrase "I am the Resurrection" from Hekat's Frog Amulet.

15. R. Graves, *The White Goddess*.

16. E. A. Wallis Budge, *The Gods of the Egyptians*.

17. J. J. Bachofen, *Myth, Religion, and Mother Right*, states that this was the Sun god Ra. Other Egyptian writings call Hathor Creatress, saying She laid the World Egg; see R. Graves, *The Greek Myths*. This myth may be the foundation for the story of the goose that laid the golden eggs.

18. E. A. Wallis Budge, *Dwellers on the Nile*.

19. Barbara Mertz, an expert in the field, says Mut should be pronounced "Moot."

20. Budge, *The Egyptian Book of the Dead*.

21. Pronounced "Noot."

22. It is not uncommon for titles and myths of goddesses to be repeated, even within the same pantheon, leaving one to wonder if these goddesses are facets of one another.

23. B. Walker, *The Woman's Encyclopedia of Myths and Secrets*.

24. James Frazer, *The Golden Bough*.

25. The symbol of Ashtart was an eight-point star. The sacred stone at Her shrine in Byblos was a meteorite.

26. M. Esther Harding, *Woman's Mysteries*.

27. Frazer, *The Golden Bough*.

28. Raphael Patai, *Myth and Modern Man*.

29. S. Angus, *The Mystery-Religions*.

30. B. Walker holds a different view on this triad. She says that Uma was pictured with a vagina dentata (teeth within the vagina); however, this symbolism should not negate Uma's position as Mother in the Hindu triad, since the vagina dentata is a patriarchal picture of the Goddess.

31. Along with Her two regular eyes, the Green Tara is shown with an eye in the center of Her forehead and one in each palm and the sole of each foot.

32. The sacred grove of Tara surrounded a stone pillar, symbolizing the regenerative power of the Goddess through union with the God.

33. Carolyne Larrington, ed., *The Feminist Companion to Mythology*.

34. B. Z. Goldberg, *The Sacred Fire*. Kuan Yin is the embodiment of the yin (female/receptive) principle.

35. To the Arabs the Sun goddess was Atthar, the Celts Sulis, the Germans Sunna, the Norwegians Sol, and the Norse Glory-of-Elves. Some of these Sun goddesses were masculinized at a later date.

36. E. O. G. Turville-Petrie, *Myth and Religion of the North*.

37. Turville-Petrie, ibid.

38. Brian Branston, *Gods of the North*.

39. The Irish word *sidh*, the Hindu *siddhi*, and the Sufi *sihr* may be of the same origin as the Norse word *seidr*.

40. In the Elder Edda, three poems, Voluspa, Baldrs Draumar, and Svipdagamal, are accounts of deceased volvas being called upon to give knowledge to the gods or protection to humans.

41. Freyja and Freyr were twin deities of sex. Freyr was a phallic god, known in Uppsala as Fricco.

42. Charles Mills Gayley, *The Classic Myths in English Literature and in Art*.

43. This fact is mentioned in the poem Oddrunargratr.

44. Charles Squire, *Celtic Myth and Legend*.

45. Squire, ibid.

46. Squire, ibid.

47. Graves, *The Greek Myths*.

48. Ross Nichols, *The Book of Druidry*.

49. Sir Thomas Malory, *Le Morte d'Arthur*. Joseph Campbell in *The Masks of God: Creative Mythology* says She was known in Germany as Cunneware.

50. H. R. Hays, *In the Beginnings*.

51. Patricia Monaghan, *The Book of Goddesses and Heroines*.

52. Erich Neumann, *The Great Mother*.

53. Neumann, ibid.

54. Joseph Campbell, *The Masks of God: Primitive Mythology*.

PART IV

Chapter 8

1. Black is not an evil color, except in the minds of certain people. To Europeans, black has long been a symbol of death; to Asians, however, white is worn to funerals.

Chapter 9

1. C. G. Jung, *The Archetypes and the Collective Unconscious*.

2. Snorri Sturluson, *The Prose Edda*.

3. J. B. Russell, *Witchcraft in the Middle Ages*.

4. E. A. Wallis Budge, *Egyptian Language*.

5. Graves, *The White Goddess*.

6. The Christian idea of vagina dentata (teeth within the vagina) probably originated from this view of the Crone. Obviously, they missed the spiritual, mystical meaning behind the image.

7. *New Larousse Encyclopedia of Mythology*.

8. Robert Graves, *The White Goddess*.

9. Whenever "virgin" priestesses had children, these were considered god-begotten. The bearing of such children gave the priestesses greater prestige in the religious and secular communities. Barbara Walker, *The Crone*.

10. Since the Hindus believed that the soul went to a place determined by its life, there were fierce Dakinis and gentle Dakinis, those who led the soul to hell and those who led the soul to heaven.

11. This included human sacrifice. There are some indications that this practice, although greatly diminished, may still be practiced today.

12. Ajit Mookerjee, *Kali: The Feminine Force*.

13. Erich Neumann, *Art and the Collective Unconscious*.

14. Budge, *The Gods of the Egyptians*.

15. E. A. Wallis Budge, *The Gods of the Egyptians*.

16. Neumann, *The Great Mother*.

17. See Chapter 3 for a more literal interpretation of this myth.

18. E. A. Wallis Budge, *Babylonian Life and History*.

19. When written of as fate goddess, the plural Gulses was used, meaning "the Fates Who Write."

20. Robert Graves, *The Greek Myths*.

21. S. Angus, *The Mystery-Religions*.

22. Graves, *The Greek Myths*.

23. Demetra George, *Mysteries of the Dark Moon*.

24. Norma Lorre Goodrich, *Priestesses*.

25. Rufus and Lawson, *Goddess Sites: Europe*.

26. Charles Squire, *Celtic Myth and Legend*.

27. *New Larousse Encyclopedia of Mythology*.

28. Lewis Spence, *The History and Origins of Druidism*.

29. Norma Lorre Goodrich, *Medieval Myths*.

30. Brian Branston, *Gods of the North*.

31. J. B. Russell, *Witchcraft in the Middle Ages*.

32. *The Woman's Encyclopedia of Myths and Secrets*.

33. Brian Branston, *Gods of the North*.

34. Turville-Petrie, *Myth and Religion of the North*.

35. R. Graves, *The White Goddess*.

36. Patricia Monaghan, *The Book of Goddesses and Heroines*.

37. Arthur Cotterell, *A Dictionary of World Mythology*.

PART V

Chapter 10

1. Sometimes this thread was golden, but more often it was said to be blood red. Erich Neumann, *The Great Mother*.

2. This triad of Fate sisters probably evolved later into the three fairy godmothers of folktales.

3. Barbara Walker, *The Woman's Dictionary of Symbols and Sacred Objects*.

4. She was shown winged or driving a chariot pulled by griffins.

5. Demetra George, *Mysteries of the Dark Moon*.

6. Ancient records say that three rough stones which fell from heaven were their images in Orchomenos.

7. The *Iliad* says that there was a whole race of Charities, of varying ages; the youngest of these was Pasithea.

8. Rufus and Lawson, *Goddess Sites: Europe*.

9. Robert Graves, *The Greek Myths*.

10. This snake-haired head was a symbol of Athene long before the patriarchal myth was written. Herodotus wrote that the matriarchal clans of the Libyan Amazons worshipped snakes as embodiments of feminine wisdom and that the female face surrounded by serpent-hair meant menstrual mysteries and Crone wisdom. Barbara Walker, *The Crone*.

11. In the tomb of a priestess of Demeter in Kertch were found hundreds of these faces made of thin gold so they could be stitched onto garments. Murray, *Who's Who in Mythology*.

12. Carolyne Larrington in *The Feminist Companion to Mythology* tells of such an instance; it protected a woman from her attacker.

13. Jennifer and Roger Woolger, *The Goddess Within*.

14. Demeter, when appearing in Her fearsome aspect as Nightmare, was said to have a black horsehead writhing with snakes.

15. The Greeks believed that anyone guilty of this crime was infected with a spiritual poison called miasma. Anyone who dared to help the guilty party also was in danger of being infected.

Notes for pages 109-122

16. Jennifer B. and Roger J. Woolger, *The Goddess Within*.

17. The Orphists called Her Eurydice (Universal Dike). The knucklebones or dice were dedicated to Her and used to select sacrificial victims. Walker, in *The Woman's Encyclopedia of Myths and Secrets*, says that Dike is an alternate spelling of Tyche.

18. Caitlin Matthews, *The Elements of The Goddess*.

19. Alexander S. Murray, *Who's Who in Mythology*.

20. Adam McLean, *The Triple Goddess*.

21. This is possibly the same black stone, the Ka'aba, now held sacred by the Moslems. It lies within the temple walls at Mecca. The Ka'aba is marked with the sign of the yoni and covered with a veil. M. Esther Harding, *Woman's Mysteries*.

22. Patricia Monaghan, *The Book of Goddesses and Heroines*.

23. Kevin Crossley-Holland, *The Norse Myths*, translates these names as Urd (Fate), Verdandi (Necessity), and Skuld (Being).

24. *New Larousse Encyclopedia of Mythology*.

25. Sometimes this spelling is Weird Sisters, meaning "fate."

26. Joseph Campbell, *The Masks of God: Creative Mythology*.

27. Barbara Walker, *The Woman's Encyclopedia of Myths and Secrets*.

Chapter 11

1. R. Graves, *The Greek Myths*.

2. Alexander Murray, *Who's Who in Mythology*.

3. Kurt Seligmann, *Magic, Supernaturalism and Religion*.

4. Barbara Walker, *The Woman's Dictionary of Symbols and Sacred Objects*.

5. Kevin Crossley-Holland, *The Norse Myths*.

Chapter 12

1. The Grimnismal says there are thirteen Valkyries, while Branston quotes other sources saying there are nine. Adam McLean writes that they most often appeared in multiples of nine, such as three nines or nine nines.

2. When in these black feathers the Valkyries were called Kraken, or crows.

3. Turville-Petrie, *Myth and Religion of the North*.

4. Joseph Campbell, *The Mythic Image*.

5. H. J. Rose, *Religion in Greece and Rome*.

6. *The Norse Myths*.

7. *The Woman's Encyclopedia of Myths and Secrets*.

8. Norma Lorre Goodrich, *Priestesses*. Goodrich says that it is possible that these women had been military officers who were quite familiar with piloting ships.

9. Gayley, *The Classic Myths in English Literature and in Art*.

PART VI

Chapter 13

1. Two of my previous books, *Celtic Magic* and *Norse Magic*, explain meditation in depth and give practical examples to follow.

2. It is now a proven scientific fact that the connecting tissue between the left and right hemispheres of the brain in women is thicker and more developed. This connecting tissue, called the *Corpus callosum*, facilitates the transactions between the two hemispheres. Gordon Rattray Taylor, *The Natural History of the Mind*.

PART VII

Chapter 15

1. Also called Uriel or Oriel.

2. For simplicity's sake, I have used the version of the power animals given in *Shamanism and the Esoteric Tradition* by Angelique S. Cook and G. A. Hawk. The chapter on Elementals in my book *The Ancient and Shining Ones* tells about the wide variety of colors used by Native Americans to designate the Quarters.

3. Traditionally, this was wine, but since many people cannot or do not care to drink any form of alcohol, it is permissible to use fruit juices or soda instead.

4. Black is not an evil color; it merely absorbs all other colors. You can, however, use dark blue or the deepest of purples if you wish.

Chapter 16

1. As in the Norse myths where Idunn was the keeper of the golden apples that kept the gods young. The same applies to Hera and Her apples of the Hesperides. The Norse called apples the sacred fruit of the gods.

2. J. E. Cirlot used this meaning, but he slants many of his interpretations to the Christian viewpoint. Pagans view sexuality as a natural thing.

3. Gertrude Jobes, *Dictionary of Mythology, Folklore and Symbols*.

4. Porphyry said that bees were the souls of priestesses. Claudia de Lys, *The Giant Book of Superstitions*.

5. The Egyptian word for cat was Mau. Budge, *The Gods of the Egyptians*.

6. Robert Graves, *The White Goddess*.

7. Science has verified that females have a certain amount of male chromosomes and hormones and males have a certain amount of female ones, the same thing the ancient Chinese knew. Jung came at this idea from a slightly different angle, calling these qualities the anima and the animus.

8. The Ouroboros was such a symbol, a dragon with its tail in its mouth. The Midgard serpent of the Norse-Germanic tales was said to hold the world together in this manner.

9. In Gaelic, shamrock is *seamrog*.

10. Barbara Walker, *The Woman's Dictionary of Symbols and Sacred Objects*. Also Joshua Trachtenberg, *Jewish Magic and Superstition: A Study in Folk Religion*.

11. Gertrude Jobes, *Dictionary of Mythology, Folklore and Symbols*, writes that Spider Woman is the weaver of fate who weaves the universe every day and unravels the web at night; when She finishes, the world will end.

12. The Christians enacted terrible penalties for worshipping at crossroads because of their connection with the Dark Mother. But they replaced the original images there with their cross which made it all right to pray at that spot.

13. Even as late as the eleventh century, Christian clergy were complaining that people still set out food and drink for the triad of sisters at the New Year. Clement A. Miles, *Christmas Customs and Traditions*.

14. Music falls under this category with the notes of the flute.

15. Harry E. Wedeck, *A Treasure of Witchcraft*.

16. Miranda Green, *The Gods of the Celts*.

17. Robert Graves, *The Greek Myths*.

18. The very ancient name of Hera was Keroessa, "Horned One," when She wore the horns of the Moon.

19. Cernunnos and Apollos Karnaios both wore horns as a sign of sexual vitality.

20. Turville-Petrie, *Myth and Religion of the North*.

21. In Ionian burials, keys were included so that the dead could unlock the gates of the underworld. In medieval times, even the Christians used keys; they temporarily put the church key under the head of the deceased so the soul would have an easy passage. Jewish midwives used to put the synagogue key in the hand of a woman in labor for an easier birth.

Notes for pages 173-192

22. W. Carew Hazlitt, *Faiths and Folklore of the British Isles*.

23. E. A. Wallis Budge, *Amulets and Talismans*.

24. Barbara Walker, *The Woman's Dictionary of Symbols and Sacred Objects*.

25. Miranda Green, *The Gods of the Celts*.

26. E. R. Ellis Davidson, *Gods and Myths of the Viking Age*. This may be tied to the word valkyrie, a female spirit of fate. The earthly representative or priestess was considered the mistress of magick knots.

27. Gertrude Jobes, *Dictionary of Mythology, Folklore and Symbols*.

28. In Ireland in particular, the geas could be taken upon oneself, like a pledge or promise. Other times it was placed on a person by someone else: a Druid, king, or the fairies.

29. W. Carew Hazlitt, *Faiths and Folklore in the British Isles*.

30. Georges Dumezil, *Archaic Roman Religion*.

31. E. O. G. Turville-Petrie, *Myth and Religion of the North*.

32. J. E. Cirlot, *A Dictionary of Symbols*.

33. Clarence P. Hornung, *Hornung's Handbook of Designs and Devices*.

34. James M. Robinson, ed., *The Nag Hammadi Library in English*.

35. A diplomatic way of saying that the three ruling gods came only through the Triple Goddess. Ernst Lehner, *Symbols, Signs and Signets*.

36. Much later, Erasmus misinterpreted the word *pithos* (vase) for *pyxis* (box) and came up with the rewritten myth of Pandora. *New Larousse Encyclopedia of Mythology*.

37. Later depictions of these goddesses did not show the wings.

BIBLIOGRAPHY

Adler, Margot. *Drawing Down the Moon*. Boston, MA: Beacon Press, 1979.

Aeschylus. 2 vols. Trans. Herbert W. Smyth. Cambridge, MA: 1952.

Aeschylus. *Eumenides*. Trans. Gilbert Murray. NY, 1925.

Aeschylus. *The "Oresteia" Trilogy and "Prometheus Bound."* Trans. Michael Townsend. San Francisco, CA: Harper and Row, 1966.

Alexander, H.B. *North American Mythology*. Mythology of All Races, vol. 10. Boston, MA: Marshall Jones, 1916.

Allen, Thomas W. and Sikes, Edward E., eds. *The Homeric Hymns*. London, UK: 1904. Second edition Oxford, 1936.

Altheim, Franz. *A History of Roman Religion*. Trans. Harold Mattingly. NY: 1938.

Altmann, Alexander. *Studies in Religious Philosophy and Mysticism*. Ithaca, 1969.

Angus, S. *The Mystery-Religions*. NY: Dover Publications, 1975.

Apuleius. *The Golden Ass*. Trans. Jack Lindsay. Indiana University Press, 1962.

Aristophanes. 3 vols. Trans. Benjamin B. Rogers. Cambridge, MA: Cambridge University Press, 1950.

Aristophanes. *The Frogs*. Trans. Richard Lattimore. NY: New American Library, 1962.

Arnott, K. *African Myths and Legends Retold*. UK: Oxford University Press, 1962.

Aswynn, Freya. *Leaves of Yggdrasil*. St. Paul, MN: Llewellyn Publications, 1990.

Athanassakis, Apostolos N., trans. *Orphic Hymns*. Scholars Press, 1977.

Avalon, Arthur. *Shakti and Shakta*. NY: Dover Publications, 1978.

Bachofen, J. J. *Myth, Religion, and Mother Right*. Edited by Joseph Campbell. Trans. Ralph Manheim. Princeton, NJ: Princeton University Press, 1973.

Baring, Anne and Cashford, Jules. *The Myth of the Goddess: Evolution of an Image*. NY: Viking Arkana, 1991.

Barthell, Edward E., Jr. *Gods and Goddesses of Ancient Greece*. Coral Gables, 1971.

Baumgartner, Anne S. *A Comprehensive Dictionary of the Gods*. NY: University Books, 1984.

Bennett, Florence Mary. *Religious Cults Associated With the Amazons*. La Rochelle, 1987. Originally published NY: 1912.

Berger, Pamela. *The Goddess Obscured: Transformation of the Grain Protectress from Goddess to Saint*. Boston, MA: Beacon Press, 1985.

Bettenson, Henry. *Livy: Rome and the Mediterranean*. NY: Penguin, 1976.

Bierhorst, John. *The Mythology of Mexico and Central America*. NY: William Morris and Co., 1990.

Blacker, Carmen. *The Catalpa Bow: A Study of Shamanistic Practices in Japan*. UK: George Allen & Unwin, 1975.

Bolen, Jean Shinoda. *Goddesses in Every Woman*. San Francisco, CA: Harper & Row, 1984.

Boulding, Elise. *The Underside of History*. Boulder, CO: Westview Press, 1976.

Branston, Brian. *Gods of the North*. London, UK: Thames & Hudson, 1955.

Branston, Brian. *The Lost Gods of England*. London, UK: Thames & Hudson, 1957.

Breasted, James H. *Development of Religion and Thought in Ancient Egypt*. NY: Charles Scribner's Sons, 1912.

Briffault, Robert. *The Mothers: A Study of the Origins of Sentiments and Institutions*, 3 vols. NY: Macmillan, 1952.

Briggs, Katherine M. *Pale Hecate's Team*. UK: Routledge & Kegan Paul, 1962.

Brown, Cheever Mackenzie. *God as Mother: A Feminine Theology in India*. Hartford, VT: Claude Stark & Co., 1974.

Budapest, Z. *The Grandmother of Time*. San Francisco, CA: Harper & Row, 1989.

Budapest, Z. *The Holy Book of Women's Mysteries*, 2 vols. Los Angeles, CA: Susan B. Anthony Coven #1, 1980.

Budapest, Z. *Selene: The Most Famous Bulleaper on Earth*. Oakland, CA: Diana Press, 1976.

Budge, E. A. Wallis. *Amulets and Superstitions*. NY: Dover Publications, 1978.

Budge, E. A. Wallis. *Babylonian Life and History*. NY: Dorset Press, 1992.

Budge, E. A. Wallis. *Dwellers on the Nile*. NY: Dover Publications, 1977.

Budge, E. A. Wallis. *The Egyptian Book of the Dead*. NY: Dover Publications, 1967.

Budge, E. A. Wallis. *Egyptian Magic*. NY: Dover Publications, 1971.

Budge, E. A. Wallis. *The Gods of the Egyptians*, 2 vols. NY: Dover Publications, 1969.

Bulfinch, Thomas. *Bulfinch's Mythology*. NY: Avenel Books, 1978.

Campbell, Florence. *Your Days are Numbered*. Ferndale, PA: The Gateway, 1975. (Originally published 1931.)

Campbell, Joseph. *The Inner Reaches of Outer Space*. NY: Harper & Row, 1986.

Campbell, Joseph. *The Masks of God: Primitive Mythology*. NY: Penguin Books, 1968.

Campbell, Joseph. *The Masks of God: Creative Mythology*. NY: Penguin Books, 1968.

Campbell, Joseph. *The Mythic Image*. NJ: Princeton University Press, 1981.

Campbell, Joseph. *Myths to Live By*. NY: Bantam Books, 1988.

Campbell, Joseph. *The Power of Myth*. NY: Doubleday, 1988.

Campbell, Joseph. *Transformation of Myth Through Time*. NY: Harper & Row, 1990.

Campbell, Joseph. *The Way of the Animal Powers*. San Francisco, CA: Harper & Row, 1983.

Campbell, Joseph and Charles Muses, eds. *In All Her Names: Explorations of the Feminine in Divinity*. San Francisco, CA: Harper & Row, 1991.

Carlyon, Richard. *A Guide to the Gods*. NY: Wm. Morrow & Co., 1982.

Cavendish, Richard, ed. *Mythology: An Illustrated Encyclopedia*. NY: Rizzoli, 1980.

Christ, Carol P. and Judith Plaskow, eds. *Womanspirit Rising: A Feminist Reader in Religion*. San Francisco, CA: Harper & Row, 1979.

Cirlot, J. E. *A Dictionary of Symbols*. NY: Philosophical Library, 1978.

Clement of Alexandria. *Exhortation to the Greeks*. Trans. G. W. Butterworth. Harvard University Press, 1919.

Clement of Alexandria. *Works*. Trans. W. Wilson. Edinburgh, 1876.

Conway, D. J. *Ancient and Shining Ones*. St. Paul, MN: Llewellyn Publications, 1993.

Conway, D. J. *Celtic Magic*. St. Paul, MN: Llewellyn Publications, 1990.

Conway, D. J. *Norse Magic*. St. Paul, MN: Llewellyn Publications, 1990.

Cook, Angelique S. and G. A. Hawk. *Shamanism and the Esoteric Tradition*. St. Paul, MN: Llewellyn Publications, 1992.

Cotterell, Arthur. *A Dictionary of World Mythology*. NY: Perigee Books, 1979.

Cotterell, Arthur, ed. *Macmillan Illustrated Encyclopedia of Myths and Legends*. NY: Macmillan, 1989.

Crawford, O. G. S. *The Eye Goddess*. NY: Macmillan, 1956.

Cumming, Charles Gordon. *The Assyrian and Hebrew Hymns of Praise*. NY: AMS Press, 1966. Originally published 1934.

Cumont, Franz. *Oriental Religions in Roman Paganism*. NY: Dover Publications, 1956.

D'Alviella, Count Goblet. *Migration of Symbols*. UK: Aquarian Press, 1979.

D'Alviella, Count Goblet. *The Mysteries of Eleusis: The Secret Rites and Rituals of the Classical Greek Mystery Tradition*. UK: Aquarian Press, 1981.

Dalley, Stephanie. *Myths From Mesopotamia: Creation, the Flood, Gilgamesh and Others*. NY: Oxford University Press, 1991.

Daly, Mary. *Beyond God the Father*. Boston, MA: Beacon Press, 1973.

Danielou, Alain. *Hindu Polytheism*. NY: Random House, 1964.

Davidson, H. R. Ellis. *Gods and Myths of Northern Europe*. NY: Bell Publishing, 1981.

Davidson, H. R. Ellis. *Gods and Myths of the Viking Age*. NY: Bell Publishing, 1981.

Davidson, H. R. Ellis. *Myths and Symbols in Pagan Europe*. Syracuse, NY: University Press, 1988.

Davies, Rodney. *Fortune-Telling With Numbers*. UK: The Aquarian Press, 1986.

de Lys, Claudia. *The Giant Book of Superstitions*. Secaucus, NJ: Citadel Press, 1979.

Diner, Helen. *Mothers and Amazons: The First Feminine History of Culture*. Trans. and ed. John Philip Lunden. NY: Doubleday/Anchor, 1973.

Doria, Charles and Harris Lenowitz, eds. *Origins: Creation Texts from the Ancient Mediterranean*. NY: Doubleday/Anchor, 1976.

Downing, Christine. *The Goddess: Mythological Images of the Feminine*. NY: Crossroad, 1984.

Driver, G. R. *Canaanite Myths and Legends*. Edinburgh: Clark, 1956.

Drury, Nevill. *The Occult Experience: Magic in the New Age*. NY: Avery Publishing Group, 1989.

Dumezil, Georges. *Archaic Roman Religion*.

Durdin-Robertson, Laurence. *The Cult of the Goddess*. Huntington Castle, Clonegal, Enniscorthy, Eire: Cesara Publications, 1974.

Durdin-Robertson, Laurence. *The Goddesses of Chaldea, Syria and Egypt*. Huntington Castle, Clonegal, Enniscorthy, Eire: Cesara Publications, 1975.

Durdin-Robertson, Laurence. *The Goddesses of India, Tibet, China and Japan*. Huntington Castle, Clonegal, Enniscorthy, Eire: Cesara Publications, 1976.

Durdin-Robertson, Laurence. *God the Mother*. Huntington Castle, Clonegal, Enniscorthy, Eire: Cesara Publications, 1982.

Ehrenfels, Omar Rolf Freiherr von. *Mother-right in India*. Oxford, 1941.

Ehrenzweig, Anton. *The Hidden Order of Art*. UK: Paladin, 1967.

Eisler, Riane. *The Chalice and the Blade: Our History, Our Future*. San Francisco, CA: Harper & Row, 1987.

Eliade, Mircea. *A History of Religious Ideas*, 3 vols. Trans. Willard R. Trask. Chicago, IL: University of Chicago Press, 1978-85.

Eliade, Mircea. *Myths, Dreams and Mysteries*. Trans. Philip Mairet. NY: Harper & Row, 1975.

Eliade, Mircea. *Rites and Symbols of Initiation*. Trans. William Trask. NY: Harper & Row, 1958.

Eliade, Mircea. *Shamanism: Archaic Techniques of Ecstasy*. Trans. William Trask. NJ: Princeton University Press, 1964.

Ellis, Hilda Roderick. *The Road to Hel*. NY: Greenwood Press, 1968.

Enheduanna. *The Exaltation of Inanna*. Trans. William H. Hallo and J. J. A. VanDijk. New Haven, CT: Yale University Press, 1968.

Euripides. 4 vols. Trans. Arthur S. Way. Cambridge, MA: Cambridge University Press, 1919, 1925, 1947.

Euripides. *The Bacchae*. Trans. William Arrowsmith. Chicago, IL: University of Chicago Press, 1959.

Evans, Sir Arthur. *The Earlier Religion of Greece in the Light of Cretan Discoveries*. UK: Macmillan, 1931.

Evans-Wentz, W. Y. *The Fairy Faith in Celtic Countries*. NY: Citadel, 1990.

Farnell, Lewis Richard. *The Cults of the Greek States*, 5 vols. Oxford, UK: Oxford University Press, 1907. Originally published 1896-1909.

Farnell, Lewis Richard. *The Higher Aspects of Greek Religion*. UK, 1912.

Farrar, Janet and Stewart. *The Witches' Goddess*. London, UK: Robert Hale, 1987.

Feinstein, David and Stanley Krippner. *Personal Mythology: The Psychology of Your Evolving Self*. UK: Jeremy P. Tarcher, 1988.

Forsdyke, Edgar John. *Greece Before Homer*. UK, 1956.

Frankfort, Henri. *Ancient Egyptian Religion*. NY: Harper & Row, Torch Books, 1961.

Frazer, James G. *The Golden Bough*. NY: Macmillan, 1963.

Gadon, Elinor W. *The Once and Future Goddess: A Symbol for our Time*. UK: Aquarian Press, 1990.

Gantz, Jeffrey, trans. *The Mabinogion*. NY: Dorset Press, 1976.

Gayley, Charles Mills. *The Classic Myths in English Literature and in Art*. NY: Ginn & Co., 1939.

George, Demetra. *Mysteries of the Dark Moon: The Healing Power of the Dark Goddess*. San Francisco, CA: Harper & Row, 1992.

Gimbutas, Marija. *The Goddesses and Gods of Old Europe, 6500-3500 BC*. Berkeley, CA: University of California Press, 1982.

Gimbutas, Marija. *The Language of the Goddess*. San Francisco, CA: Harper & Row, 1989.

Godwin, Joscelyn. *Mystery Religions in the Ancient World*. UK: Thames & Hudson, 1981.

Goldberg, B. Z. *The Sacred Fire*. NY: University Books, 1958.

Goldberg, Herb. *The Hazards of Being Male*. NY: Signet, 1977.

Goldenberg, Naomi R. *Changing of the Gods*. Boston, MA: Beacon Press, 1979.

Goodman, Morris C. *Modern Numerology*. No. Hollywood, CA: Wilshire Book Co., 1974.

Goodrich, Norma Lorre. *Ancient Myths*. NY: New American Library, 1960.

Goodrich, Norma Lorre. *Medieval Myths*. NY: New American Library, 1977.

Goodrich, Norma Lorre. *Priestesses*. NY: HarperCollins, 1989.

Grant, Frederick Clifton, ed. and trans. *Hellenistic Religions: The Age of Syncretism*. NY: Macmillan, 1953.

Graves, Robert. *The Greek Myths*. UK: Penguin, 1961.

Graves, Robert. *The White Goddess*. NY: Farrar, Straus & Giroux, 1980.

Gray, John. *Near Eastern Mythology*. UK: Hamlyn, 1982.

Gray, Louis Herbert, ed. *The Mythology of All Races*, 7 vols. Boston, MA: 1916.

Gray, William G. *Evoking the Primal Goddess*. St. Paul, MN: Llewellyn Publications, 1989.

Green, Miranda. *The Gods of the Celts*. Totowa, NJ: Barnes & Noble, 1986.

Grey, Sir George. *Polynesian Mythology: An Ancient Traditional History of the New Zealand Race, as Furnished by Their Priests and Chiefs*. UK: Whitcombe & Tombs, 1929. Originally published 1855.

Guirand, Felix, ed. *New Larousse Encyclopedia of Mythology*. Trans. Richard Aldington and Delano Ames. UK: Hamlyn, 1978.

Guterbock, Hans G. *Mythologies of the Ancient World*. Ed. Samuel N. Kramer. Chicago, IL: 1961.

Hall, Manly P. *The Secret Teachings of All Ages*. Los Angeles, CA: Philosophical Research Society, 1977.

Hall, Nor. *The Moon and the Virgin*. San Francisco, CA: Harper & Row, 1980.

Hamilton, Edith. *Mythology*. Boston, MA: Little, Brown & Co., 1942.

Harding, M. Esther. *Woman's Mysteries, Ancient and Modern*. NY: Bantam, 1973.

Harrison, Jane Ellen. *Ancient Art and Ritual*. UK: 1913.

Harrison, Jane Ellen. *Mythology*. NY: Harcourt Brace & World, 1963.

Harrison, Jane Ellen. *Myths of Greece and Rome*. UK: Ernest Benn Ltd., 1927.

Harrison, Jane Ellen. *Prolegomena to the Study of Greek Religion*. UK: Merlin Press, 1980.

Harrison, Jane Ellen. *The Religion of Ancient Greece*. UK: Archibald Constable & Co., 1905.

Harrison, Jane Ellen. *Themis: A Study of the Social Origins of Greek Religion*. UK: Merlin Press, 1963.

Hawkes, Jacquetta. *Dawn of the Gods: Minoan and Mycenaeon Origins of Greece*. NY: Random House, 1968.

Hays, H. R. *In the Beginnings*. NY: G. P. Putnam's Sons, 1963.

Hazlitt, W. Carew. *Faiths and Folklore in the British Isles*.

Heline, Corinne. *Sacred Science of Numbers*. Los Angeles, CA: New Age Press, 1977.

Herodotus. 4 vols. Trans. A. D. Godley. NY, 1920.

Herodotus. *The Histories*. Trans. Aubrey de Selincourt. NY: Penguin, 1954.

Herzberg, Max J. *Myths and Their Meaning*. Boston, MA: Allyn & Bacon, 1928.

Hesiod. *The Homeric Hymns*. Trans. H. G. Evelyn-White. Heinemann, 1964.

Hesiod. *Hesiod and Theognis*. Ed. E. V. Rieu. UK: 1973.

Hesiod. *The Homeric Hymns and Homerica*. Trans. H. G. Evelyn-White. Cambridge, MA: Cambridge University Press, 1959.

Hesiod. *"Theogony" and "Works and Days."* Trans. Dorothea Wender. UK: Penguin, 1973.

Hillman, James, ed. *Facing the Gods*. TX: Spring Publications, 1980.

Hippolytus. *Refutation of All Heresies*. Trans. Werner Foerster. Gnosis, 1971.

Hooke, S. H. *Babylonian and Assyrian Religion*. UK: Hutchinson, 1953.

Hornung, Clarence P. *Hornung's Handbook of Designs and Devices*. NY: Dover Publications, 1959.

Howell, James. *Dodona's Grove*. Cambridge, MA: Cambridge University Press, 1945.

Hultkrantz, Ake. *The Religions of the American Indians*. Berkeley, CA: University of California Press, 1979.

Iamblichus of Chalcis. *Iamblichus on The Mysteries of the Egyptians, Chaldeans, and Assyrians*. Trans. Thomas Taylor. UK: 1821, 1895, 1968.

James, E. O. *The Ancient Gods*. NY: Putnam, 1960.

James, E. O. *The Cult of the Mother-Goddess: An Archaeological and Documentary Study*. NY: Frederick A. Praeger, 1959.

Jayakar, Pupul. *The Earth Mother: Legends, Ritual Arts and Goddesses of India*. San Francisco, CA: Harper & Row, 1989.

Jobes, Gertrude. *Dictionary of Mythology, Folklore and Symbols*. NY: Scarecrow Press, 1962.

Johnson, Buffie. *Lady of the Beasts: Ancient Images of the Goddess and Her Sacred Animals*. San Francisco, CA: Harper & Row, 1988.

Johnson, Robert A. *He—Understanding Masculine Psychology*. San Francisco, CA: Harper & Row, 1977.

Johnson, Robert A. *She—Understanding Feminine Psychology*. San Francisco, CA: Harper & Row, 1977.

Jonas, H. *The Gnostic Religion*. Boston, MA: Beacon Press, 1963.

Jung, Carl G. *The Archetypes and the Collective Unconscious*. Princeton, NJ: Princeton University Press, 1990.

Jung, Carl G. *Psychology and Religion: West and East*. NJ: Princeton University Press, 1969.

Jung, Carl G. and Kerenyi, C. *The Myth of the Divine Child*. NJ: Princeton University Press, 1973.

Jung, Emma and Marie-Louise von Franz. *The Grail Legend*. NY: Putnam, 1970.

Kerenyi, Karl. *Athene: Virgin and Mother in Greek Religion*. Trans. Murray Stein. Houston, TX: Spring Publications, 1978.

Kerenyi, Karl. *Eleusis: Archetypal Image of Mother and Daughter*. NY: Schocken Books, 1967.

Kerenyi, Karl. *Goddesses of Sun and Moon*. Trans. Murray Stein. Dallas, TX: Spring Publications, 1979.

Kerenyi, Karl. *The Gods of the Greeks*. Trans. Norman Cameron. UK: Thames and Hudson, 1979.

Kerenyi, Karl. *The Religion of the Greeks and Romans*. Trans. Christopher Holme. NY: Penguin, 1962.

Kerenyi, Karl. *Zeus and Hera: Archetypal Image of Father, Husband and Wife*. Trans. Christopher Holme. Princeton, NJ: Princeton University Press, 1975.

Kinsley, David R. *The Sword and the Flute: Kali and Krsna, Dark Visions of the Terrible and the Sublime in Hindu Mythology*. Berkeley, CA: University of California Press, 1975.

Kitagawa, Joseph M. *Religion in Japanese History*. NY: Columbia University Press, 1966.

Knight, Gareth. *The Rose Cross and the Goddess*. NY: Destiny Books, 1985.

Koltuv, Barbara Black. *The Book of Lilith*. York Beach, ME: Nicolas-Hays, Inc., 1986.

Kramer, Samuel N. *Sumerian Mythology: A Study of Spiritual and Literary Achievement in the Third Millennium BC*. Philadelphia, PA: University of Pennsylvania, 1972.

Kramer, Samuel N. *The Sumerians: Their History, Culture and Character*. Chicago, IL: University of Chicago Press, 1963.

Lang, Andrew. *Myth, Ritual and Religion*. 2 vols. UK, 1901.

Larrington, Carolyne, ed. *The Feminist Companion to Mythology*. UK: Pandora, 1992.

Lehner, Ernst. *Symbols, Signs and Signets*. NY: Dover Publications, 1950.

Lethaby, W. R. *Architecture, Mysticism and Myth*. NY: George Braziller, 1975.

Levy, G. Rachel. *The Gate of Horn: A Study of the Religious Conceptions of the Stone Age and Their Influence upon European Thought*. UK: Faber & Faber, 1946.

Livy. *History of Rome*. Trans. Henry Bettenson. NY: Penguin, 1976.

Lloyd, Seton. *Early Anatolia*. UK: 1961.

Lovelock, James. *Gaia: A New Look at Life on Earth*. Oxford: Oxford University Press, 1979.

Lucian. *Menippus*. Trans. A. M. Harmon. Harvard University Press, The Loeb Classical Library, 1925.

Lucian. *Selected Satires of Lucian*. Trans. Lionel Casson. NY: Doubleday, 1962.

Lucian. *The Syrian Goddess*. Trans. Harold W. Attridge and Robert A. Oden. Scholars Press, 1976.

Lumholtz, Carl. *Unknown Mexico: A Record of 5 Years' Exploration among the Tribes of the Western Sierra Madre in the 'tierra caliente' of Tepic and Jalisco and among the Tarascos of Michoacan*. NY: 1903.

Lurker, Manfred. *Dictionary of Gods and Goddesses, Devils and Demons*. NY: Routledge & Kegan Paul, 1987.

MacCanna, Proinsias. *Celtic Mythology*. NY: Peter Bedrick Books, 1983.

MacCulloch, J. A. *The Celtic and Scandinavian Religions*. Westport, CT: Greenwood Press, 1973.

MacCulloch, John Arnott. *The Mythology of All Races*, 13 vols. Boston, MA: 1918.

Malory, Sir Thomas. *Le Morte d'Arthur*. UK: J. M. Dent & Sons Ltd., 1961.

Marinatos, Spyridon. *Crete and Mycenae*. NY: Harry N. Abrams, 1960.

Markale, Jean. *Women of the Celts*. London, UK: Cremonesi, 1975.

Matthews, Caitlin. *The Elements of the Celtic Tradition*. UK: Element Books, 1989.

Matthews, Caitlin. *The Elements of the Goddess*. UK: Element Books, 1989.

Matthews, John. *The Arthurian Tradition*. Rockport, MA: Element Books, 1989.

Matthews, John. *Taliesin: Shamanism and the Bardic Mysteries in Britain and Ireland*. UK: Aquarian Press, 1991.

Matthews, John and Caitlin. *The Aquarian Guide to British and Irish Mythology*. UK: Aquarian Press, 1988.

McLean, Adam. *The Triple Goddess: An Exploration of the Archetypal Feminine*. Grand Rapids, MI: Phanes Press, 1989.

Mertz, Barbara. *Temples, Tombs and Hieroglyphs*. NY: Dodd, Mead & Co., 1978.

Meyer, Marvin W., ed. *The Ancient Mysteries: A Sourcebook*. San Francisco, CA: Harper & Row, 1987.

Miles, Clement A. *Christmas Customs and Traditions*.

Monaghan, Patricia. *The Book of Goddesses and Heroines*. St. Paul, MN: Llewellyn Publications, 1990.

Mookerjee, Ajit. *Kali: The Feminine Force*. Rochester, VT: Destiny Books, 1988.

Morganwg, Iolo, ed. *The Triads of Britain*. London, UK: Wildwood House, 1977.

Murray, Alexander S. *Who's Who in Mythology*. NY: Bonanza Books, 1988.

Mylonas, George. *Eleusis and the Eleusinean Mysteries*. NJ: Princeton University Press, 1961.

Mylonas, George E. *The Hymn to Demeter and Her Sanctuary at Eleusis*. St. Louis: Washington University Language and Literature Series, #13, 1942.

Mylonas, George E. *Mycenae and the Mycenaean Age*. Princeton, NJ: Princeton University Press, 1966.

Neumann, Erich. *The Great Mother: An Analysis of the Archetype*. Princeton, NJ: Princeton University Press, 1974.

Nichols, Ross. *The Book of Druidry*. UK: Aquarian Press, 1991.

Nilsson, Martin P. *Greek Popular Religion*. NY: Columbia University Press, 1947.

Nilsson, Martin P. *The Minoan-Mycenaean Religion and its Survival in Greek Religion*. NY: Biblo & Tannen, 1971.

Olson, Carl, ed. *The Book of the Goddess Past and Present*. NY: Crossroad, 1989.

Otto, Walter. *The Homeric Gods*. Boston, MA: Beacon Press, 1964.

Panofsky, Dora and Erwin. *Pandora's Box*. NJ: Princeton University Press, 1962.

Parrinder, Geoffrey. *A Dictionary of Non-Christian Religions*. Philadelphia, PA: Westminster Press, 1971.

Patai, Raphael. *The Hebrew Goddess*. NY: Avon, 1978.

Patai, Raphael. *Myth and Modern Man*. Englewood Cliffs, NJ: Prentice-Hall, 1972.

Pausanias. *Description of Greece*, books 4 and 6. Trans. W.H.S. Jones & H. A. Omerod. Harvard University Press, The Loeb Classical Library, 1926-1933.

Perera, Sylvia Brinton. *Descent to the Goddess: A Way of Initiation for Women*. Canada: Inner City Books, 1981.

Persson, Axel Waldemar. *The Religion of Greece in Prehistoric Times*. Los Angeles, CA: 1942.

Plato. *The Republic*. Trans. Desmond Lee. NY: Penguin, 1955.

Poignant, Roslyn. *Oceanic Mythology: The Myths of Polynesia, Micronesia, Melanesia, Australia*. UK: Paul Hamlyn, 1975.

Pomeroy, Sarah B. *Goddesses, Whores, Wives and Slaves: Women in Classical Antiquity*. NY: Schocken Books, 1975.

Pritchard, James B., ed. *The Ancient Near East: An Anthology of Texts and Pictures*, 2 vols. NJ: Princeton University Press, 1958.

Pritchard, James B. *Palestinian Figurines in Relation to Certain Goddesses Known through Literature*. American Oriental Society, 1943.

Prudentius. *Cybele and Attis*. Trans. Maarten J. Vermaseren. UK: Thames & Hudson, 1977.

Purce, Jill. *The Mystic Spiral: Journey of the Soul*. NY: Thames & Hudson, 1974.

Reed, Ellen Cannon. *The Witches' Qabala: The Goddess and the Tree*. St. Paul, MN: Llewellyn Publications, 1985.

Rees, Alwyn and Brinley. *Celtic Heritage*. NY: Grove Press, 1961.

Rice, David G. and John E. Stambaugh, trans. *Sources for the Study of Greek Religion*. Scholars Press, 1979.

Richardson, Emmeline. *The Etruscans*. Chicago, IL: 1964.

Ringgren, Helmer. *Religions of the Ancient Near East*. Trans. John Sturdy. Philadelphia, PA: Westminster Press, 1973.

Robertson, J. M. *Pagan Christs*. NY: Dorset Press, 1966.

Robinson, James M., ed. *The Nag Hammadi Library in English*. San Francisco, CA: Harper & Row, 1977.

Rose, H. J. *Religion in Greece and Rome*. NY: Harper & Row, 1959.

Ross, Anne. *Pagan Celtic Britain*. London, UK: Routledge & Kegan Paul, 1967.

Rufus, Anneli S. and Kristan Lawson. *Goddess Sites: Europe*. San Francisco, CA: Harper & Row, 1991.

Russel, J. B. *Witchcraft in the Middle Ages*. Ithaca, NY: Cornell University Press, 1972.

Sandars, N. K., ed. *Poems of Heaven and Hell from Ancient Mesopotamia*. UK: Penguin, 1972.

Seligmann, Kurt. *Magic, Supernaturalism, and Religion*. NY: Pantheon Books, 1948.

Sharkey, John. *Celtic Mysteries: The Ancient Religion*. NY: The Crossroad Publishing Co., 1975.

Shore, Lesley. *Reclaiming Woman's Voice: Becoming Whole*. St. Paul, MN: Llewellyn Publications, 1992.

Shuttle, Penelope and Redgrove, Peter. *The Wise Wound: Menstruation and Everywoman*. UK: Paladin, 1986.

Singer, June. *Androgyny: Toward a New Theory of Sexuality*. NY: Anchor Press, 1976.

Sjoo, Monica and Mor, Barbara. *The Great Cosmic Mother: Rediscovering the Religion of the Earth*. San Francisco, CA: Harper & Row, 1987.

Slater, Philip E. *The Glory of Hera: Greek Mythology and the Greek Family*. Boston, MA: Beacon Press, 1968.

Smith, John Holland. *The Death of Classical Paganism*. NY: Scribner, 1976.

Smith, Morton. *Clement of Alexandria and a Secret Gospel of Mark*. Cambridge, MA: Harvard University Press, 1973.

Sobol, Donald J. *The Amazons of Greek Mythology*. Cranbury, NJ: A. S. Barnes & Co., 1972.

Sophocles. Trans. F. Storr. Cambridge, MA: The Loeb Library, 1951.

Spence, Lewis. *An Encyclopedia of Occultism*. NY: University Books, 1960.

Spence, Lewis. *The History and Origins of Druidism*. NY: Samuel Weiser, 1971.

Spence, Lewis. *The Magic Arts in Celtic Britain*. NY: Dorset Press, 1992.

Spence, Lewis. *The Mysteries of Britain: Secret Rites and Traditions of Ancient Britain*. London, UK: Rider & Co., 1979.

Spretnak, Charlene. *Lost Goddesses of Early Greece: A Collection of Pre-Hellenic Myths*. Boston, MA: Beacon Press, 1992.

Squire, Charles. *Celtic Myth and Legend, Poetry and Romance*. NY: Bell Publishing Co., 1979.

Starhawk. *The Spiral Dance*. NY: Harper & Row, 1979.

Stein, Diane. *Stroking the Python*. St. Paul, MN: Llewellyn Publications, 1988.

Stein, Diane. *The Women's Spirituality Book*. St. Paul, MN: Llewellyn Publications, 1987.

Stepanich, Kisma K. *The Gaia Tradition: Celebrating the Earth in Her Seasons*. St. Paul, MN: Llewellyn Publications, 1991.

Stepanich, Kisma K. *Sister Moon Lodge: The Power and Mystery of Menstruation*. St. Paul, MN: Llewellyn Publications, 1992.

Stewart, R. J. *Celtic Gods, Celtic Goddesses*. UK: Blandford, 1990.

Stewart, R. J. *The Underworld Initiation: A Journey Towards Psychic Transformation*. UK: Aquarian Press, 1985.

Stone, Merlin. *Ancient Mirrors of Womanhood*. Boston, MA: Beacon Press, 1984.

Stone, Merlin. *Heroine Lore from Around the World*. Boston, MA: Beacon Press, 1984.

Stone, Merlin. *When God Was a Woman*. NY: Harcourt Brace Jovanovich, 1976.

Strayhorn, Lloyd. *Numbers and You*. NY: Ballantine Books, 1987.

Sturluson, Snorri. *The Prose Edda*. Berkeley, CA: University of California Press, 1954.

Suhr, Elmer G. *The Spinning Aphrodite: The Evolution of the Goddess from Earliest Pre-Hellenic Symbolism through Late Classical Times*. NY: Helios Books, 1969.

Taylor, Gordon Rattray. *The Natural History of the Mind*. NY: E. P. Dutton, 1979.

Thompson, S. *Tales of the North American Indians*. Cambridge, MA: Harvard University Press, 1929.

Thomson, George. *The Prehistoric Aegean*. NY: The Citadel Press, 1965.

Trachtenberg, Joshua. *Jewish Magic and Superstition: A Study of Folk Religion*.

Turville-Petre, E. O. G. *Myth and Religion of the North*. NY: Holt, Rinehart & Winston, 1964.

Vermaseren, Maarten J. *Cybele and Attis: The Myth and the Cult.* Trans. A.M.H. Lemmers. UK: Thames and Hudson, 1977.

Waddell, L. Austine. *Tibetan Buddhism.* NY: Dover Publications, 1972.

Wainwright, F. T. *Scandinavian England.* Sussex, UK: Phillimore & Co., 1975.

Walker, Barbara G. *The Crone: Woman of Age, Wisdom and Power.* San Francisco, CA: Harper & Row, 1985.

Walker, Barbara G. *The Woman's Dictionary of Symbols and Sacred Objects.* San Francisco, CA: Harper & Row, 1988.

Walker, Barbara G. *The Woman's Encyclopedia of Myths and Secrets.* San Francisco, CA: Harper & Row, 1983.

Warner, Rex. *The Stories of the Greeks.* NY: Farrar, Straus & Giroux, 1967.

Ward, Marina. *Alone of All Her Sex: The Myth and Cult of the Virgin Mary.* UK: Pan Books, 1985.

Waters, Frank. *Book of the Hopi.* NY: Ballantine Books, 1976.

Wedeck, Harry E. *A Treasury of Witchcraft.* Secaucus, NJ: Citadel Press, 1975.

Weigle, Marta. *Spiders and Spinsters: Women and Mythology.* Albuquerque, NM: University of New Mexico Press, 1982.

Whitmont, Edward C. *The Return of the Goddess.* NY: Crossroads, 1982.

Wilkin, Robert Louis. *The Christians as the Romans Saw Them.* New Haven, CT: 1984.

Willetts, R. F. *Cretan Cults and Festivals.* UK: Routledge & Kegan Paul, 1962.

Wolfe, Amber. *In the Shadow of the Shaman.* St. Paul, MN: Llewellyn Publications, 1988.

Wolkstein, Diane and Kramer, Samuel N. *Inanna, Queen of Heaven and Earth: Her Stories and Hymns from Sumer.* UK: Rider & Co., 1983.

Woolger, Jennifer B. and Roger J. *The Goddess Within: A Guide to the Eternal Myths that Shape Women's Lives.* NY: Fawcett Columbine, 1989.

Zimmer, Heinrich. *Myths and Symbols in Indian Art and Civilization.* Princeton, NJ: Princeton University Press, 1946.

Zolla, Elemire. *The Androgyne: Reconciliation of Male and Female.* NY: Crossroads, 1981.

Zuntz, Gunther. *Persephone: Three Essays on Religion and Thought in Magna Graecia.* UK: Oxford University Press, 1971.

INDEX